First Pentecostal Church
1110 Belleton ~ Road
Flatwoods, KY 41139

Rehumanize
INTERNATIONAL
309 Smithfield Street STE 210
Pittsburgh PA, 15222
740-963-9565   www.rehumanizeintl.org

WAYWARD SOLDIER

**A Reserve Psychologist's Memoir and Analysis
During the Second American-Iraqi War**

Dr. Mark J. Hovee, Psy.D.
September 8, 2006

ISBN 0-7414-3648-5

Published by:

INFINITY
PUBLISHING.COM

1094 New DeHaven Street, Suite 100
West Conshohocken, PA 19428-2713
Info@buybooksontheweb.com
www.buybooksontheweb.com
Toll-free (877) BUY BOOK
Local Phone (610) 941-9999
Fax (610) 941-9959

Printed in the United States of America

Printed on Recycled Paper

Published February 2007

DISCLAIMER: The views expressed are solely those of the author and do not reflect the official policy or position of the Department of the Army, the Department of Defense or the government of the United States of America. Other than researched portions of Chapters 2 and 7, the observations and analyses are subjective and reflective in nature, and are therefore not guided by the rigors of objective inquiry. However, the author has made every attempt to represent all the events and statements by individuals as accurately as possible, avoiding any assumptions or conclusions which stretch beyond what actually occurred or has been stated. E-mail correspondence is provided whenever possible to establish an authentic record of the views and statements by individuals, as well as dialogue between parties.

The opinions, convictions, assertions, and non-researched theories promoted by the author should not be construed as having any objectively or empirically derived validity. These are rather the views belonging solely to the author in keeping with the highly personal and subjective content of a memoir.

The author's vocation as a clinical psychologist does not imply any additional legitimacy or expertise to his ideas and opinions beyond what could be expected from other soldiers lacking training in psychology. It is left entirely in the reader's mind to determine what portions of the book ring true or resonant with him or her, if any, and what ones do not.

TABLE OF CONTENTS

Acknowledgements

There are a number of individuals who are very deserving of being acknowledged. First and foremost would be my wife, Judy, who so patiently tolerated the hours on end I spent at the computer. She was also very affirming in the countless times she listened to me read portions of the manuscript, not to mention the plethora of occasions where I waxed not so eloquent on some facet of the book in progress. I am eternally grateful for her steadfast support without which I very likely would not have prevailed to the finish line.

My three children (i.e. Nate, Maris and Claire) also deserve special recognition in that they stood by me during my absence from them for a year of Army duty in Germany. It was during this lonely period that the experiences occurred, and the ideas formulated, which ultimately led to this finished product. Each of them in their own endearing ways contributed to this book. They would at times hear me out, as I expounded on some aspect of the manuscript, and on one occasion allowed me to read a portion to all of them at the same time. Unbeknownst to them, they continued to serve as a tremendous source of inspiration in helping me forward with the "great project."

A year ago in the summer, I spent some time with my family of origin back in Washington State. It was during this time that I shared many aspects of my partially written manuscript with my mother and two brothers, Eric and Dan, along with Eric's wife, Beth, and Dan's significant other, Sharon. They all provided helpful feedback and support.

This trip was culminated by a presentation I gave at a local church there regarding my work with soldiers and spouses in Germany. The attendance of my spouse and children, my family of origin, my cousin, Julie, and a couple of long time friends, David Hawley and Dan Hansen, all meant a great deal to me. Their willingness to hear me out instilled in me a more steely determination to continue plumbing the depths of my experiences – that there was something worth sharing and ultimately leading to a permanent record in written form.

I am extremely indebted to a colleague, Dr. Brad Johnson, Ph.D., who scrutinized portions of the manuscript at various stages in the process. His ongoing support of my writing endeavors repeatedly bolstered me to continue on, even at points where it seemed like I was "dying on the vine." He has acquired specialized knowledge and expertise of military matters that proved invaluable in guiding me through the turbulent waters associated with the book's content. He possesses a unique quality from the ranks of true academics in terms of availability, openness and genuinely kind disposition. He has been a tremendous encourager for me to proceed forward with daunting challenges that otherwise would seem insurmountable. He has truly been a "class act" in the best sense of the word.

Many pieces of the puzzle which resulted in this completed work are attributable to the fine staff I worked with at Landstuhl Regional Medical Center and at Baumholder Health Clinic in Germany. Their candor regarding a host of issues in the military assisted me significantly with some of the ideas developed in the book. The poignancy of some of their struggles connected to the war had a deep impact on me, and has worked its way into my own thinking and writing.

The soldiers and spouses I worked with in Germany, most notably with the Armored Brigade at Baumholder, certainly played a key role in the making of this book. Their willingness to share the many traumas and difficult times they encountered both in Germany and the Middle East served considerably to crystallize ideas in my mind. Their tremendous sacrifices and courage served as a form of inspiration that compelled me to move forward in documenting what they went through individually and collectively.

Within their ranks, I want to acknowledge in particular a clinical psychologist, Captain Matthew Ubben, who willingly provided many insights into his experiences in Iraq as a mental health provider. I will always be grateful to his transparency which has leaked its way onto the pages of this book. He also is responsible for proofing the chapter which focused on soldiers and spouses at Landstuhl and Baumholder.

Finally, I want to acknowledge the strenuous efforts and enormous sacrifices made by American, British and other coalition forces in Afghanistan and Iraq. This includes the other foreign workers in these countries, whether they be with the media, contract workers, missionaries, relief workers and so forth – many of whom gave so much of themselves in trying to improve conditions for Iraqis, Afghanis, and coalition forces. Additionally, I acknowledge many of the Iraqi and Afghani citizens who have suffered so much during the war, and have experienced so many personal losses. I could not have written this book without having been so deeply moved by the level of suffering and anguish experienced by all these groups in Iraq and Afghanistan.

CHAPTER 1
INTRODUCTION

Every American now serving in harm's way at some point voluntarily chose military service. Many of them did not realize they would be serving in Iraq; many National Guardsmen and reservists did not imagine they would be plucked out of civilian life for sustained tours overseas...The administration constantly says the nation is "at war," but of course it is not. The tiny fraction of Americans who are in uniform have been hard pressed in the years since 9/11. Thousands have been killed; tens of thousands injured; hundreds of thousands sent overseas for months on end (Fallows, 2006 p.227).

With their tormented stories and emotional breakdowns, the winter soldiers investigation was incredibly powerful. "It was a mindblower," Butler recalled. "It was extraordinary. With my background I couldn't imagine a soldier saying, 'I've done wrong.' I couldn't imagine people expressing hatred of the war so articulately—in my opinion what ended the war in Vietnam was the veterans. Once the troops spoke out against it you couldn't fight the war much longer" (Brinkley, 2004, pp. 349-350).

World history, it seemed, was like one endless panoramic of Picasso's Guernica, where the sword always ruled. "War as always contrasted the real with the absurd—unless someone was in love with what they were doing and then there was a reasoning for everything—even dying" (Brinkley, 2004, p. 351).

It was not my intention to write a book about the war with Iraq. This seemed better suited to prolific writers with a natural leaning for military history and political science. They would most adequately chronicle the host of events leading up to the war, the prosecution of the war itself, and the post-war developments for Iraq, the Middle-East as a whole, and the allied forces. I have enough of an understanding of these disciplines to recognize my limitations.

But, I could not steer clear of the fact that I had personally been impacted by the terrorist attacks of September 11, 2001 and the subsequent sequence of events leading to the second American-Iraqi war. This of course could be so stated by millions of people in the United States and many other parts of the world as well. It would be rather unusual not to be affected by the magnitude of this terrorist assault on U.S. soil, and the actions taken by the American government in response.

In a rather eclectic manner, the chapters of this book reveal some seminal experiences I have had at different points since 9/11, and especially since the war with Iraq commenced. This includes some researched content, particularly with respect to a chapter devoted to salient psychological factors associated to the Abu Ghraib debacle.

It has been my endeavor to provide the reader with some windows allowing for differing observation points from which to grasp pieces of my thinking about a very troubling war. In addition, it has been my intention to highlight facets of myself as a psychologist, soldier, American citizen, and human being – one lacking many of the answers being sought after and one quite predisposed to struggling with ambiguities.

I have attempted to capture herein the essential issues of the war years in accordance with my own thoughts, impressions and analysis. I will be the first to acknowledge that some of my views may be quite unique, and possibly unsettling, when compared with the norms of civilians and military personnel alike. This being noted, the aim has been to bring such views into the open sufficiently, and to provide readers with varied enough material to encourage further investigation of their own.

It is incumbent on me to exercise the democratic principles espoused in this book in order to truly allow for unlimited critiques of this book along with proposed alterations. Also, this is but one book on a very broad topic that has impacted most American lives to some extent. It is to be expected that some readers may delve much deeper into certain topics noted in the book through their own research, and this is to be applauded.

As the title suggests, my views on soldiering may be found to be quite distinct and unorthodox from what people generally conclude about the military profession. This is likely more telling by virtue of my ongoing commitment to the Army Reserve. If I had resigned my commission, then my voice might not sound so different from other retired military who consider themselves free to express their true opinions about the military. However, since I remain active in the Reserves, the notions and personal sentiments made public in this book tend to appear more unusual and non-conformist to standard protocol.

If I can actually be classified as a "wayward soldier," it would probably be due to the facets of soldiering that I emphasize. I tend to be very sensitive to how other soldiers are treated, and conversely how soldiers treat those they have some control over. Humane treatment of all people regardless of their actions against American soldiers is extremely high on my priority list.

Conversely, my deviance from the norm shares a kindred spirit with a number of discharged soldiers who have spoken out about the military issues they previously thought were off limits for active duty personnel. These grievances primarily tend to revolve around the way soldiers are properly protected and cared for along with the manner in which a war is being prosecuted in as effective and humane approach as possible.

My concern for the mental-emotional wellbeing of all persons, especially those I provide services for, is not just an outgrowth of my training, but additionally due to the importance I naturally render to human needs on multiple levels. Unlike a common military perspective of toughness and disregard of psychological needs, I consider these areas to be critical items to focus on. In combat situations, the maintenance of respect for human life and humane treatment of fellow soldiers remain essential attitudes that I believe should be cultivated in soldiers.

The action of freely speaking one's mind - whether this be mere opinions, knowledge from personal experience and/ or more systematic research findings – serves as one of the main features in this book. The focus is particularly oriented toward the exercising of free speech in the armed forces. The constraints placed on soldiers in expressing their viewpoints, even about the war they are a part of, is probed in considerable depth.

My own unpleasant encounter with limitations placed on academic liberties to publish while on active duty provides some much needed insight into this facet of military life. It has been my endeavor to demonstrate firsthand the negative fallout from such rigid control, not just for myself, but more importantly for the entire military institution. The tradition bound paradigm which calls for tight scrutiny and oversight of proposed manuscripts, and free speech in general, is challenged in part for its prevention of "checks and balances" of military operations and behavior up and down the "chain of command."

The reader will be confronted with fundamental questions regarding human rights in a free society. As suggested in this book, these are issues which may be central to the practical application of democratic principles in our country, especially as it relates to the military use of force and the degree to which such intervention impacts the lives of soldiers and noncombatants.

The shaping and redirecting of governmental policies toward the war in Iraq will be influenced to a greater or lesser extent by the degree to which the reasoned voices of enlisted soldiers and officers can be tolerated. Having wrestled with the freedom of speech dilemma for over two years now, I have become more convinced than ever that the prosecution of this war, as well as wars to come, is significantly molded by the way this constitutional problem is handled.

My prompting to write about various aspects of the war years, mostly from an experiential standpoint, came to fruition through my year deployment to Germany with the Army. It is unlikely the impetus to piece together this book would have ever materialized without this year stint of working with soldiers and spouses at Landstuhl, Germany. My "hands on" work there as an Army psychologist laid the foundation for this present publication, as I was exposed to so many unforgettable encounters with soldiers, spouses, and the staff I worked with. It was out of this array of emotion-packed experiences and discussions with so many themselves struggling with war related issues that the urge to write began to take hold. It struck me as such a waste for all of the poignancy of these intense human encounters during a seminal period of American history to remain unrecorded.

What I had at my disposal during the year of familial exile in Germany was ample opportunity to hear about the war in Iraq from numerous soldiers coming back from the Iraqi and

Afghani theaters. Prior to the return of a large number of these soldiers, my job specifically brought me into near daily therapy sessions with spouses anxiously awaiting the return of their soldier spouses "downrange." I also had the opportunity to talk with many soldiers stationed in Germany who harbored their own views about the war, some which were verbally shared and much that remained unspoken. Communication with professional colleagues (i.e. such as psychiatrists, other psychologists, and social workers) was another feature available to me over the course of the year. I felt fortunate to hear some of their uncensored attitudes and thoughts about the war and its impact on American soldiers they treated. The input of local Germans and other European civilians living in and around Germany was additionally very valuable in providing other perspectives of the Iraq war.

Not only was it possible to hyper-focus on war issues with so many varied groups and individual personalities, but my job allowed for considerable "free time" to think through the many verbalized experiences and notions. I actually had the luxury, if it can be called that, of processing so much I had been exposed to in an attempt to make sense of it. If I was not meditating on some of this while driving numerous hours to other European destinations on weekends, I would likely be found engaging in similar contemplation at my office computer terminal within the hospital.

Still, my resolve to begin writing during this year away could not have been realized without a growing level of frustration and anger about the war. The surprising truth that I had to contend with was that the realities of the war had been taking a toll on me. As much as I tried to remain dispassionate in my role as a clinical psychologist, what continued to occur with American soldiers and spouses, Iraqis, insurgents, and the Middle East at large became increasingly more difficult to keep compartmentalized. I was having a harder time finding any significant purpose for prosecuting a war which was having such devastating impact on the lives of so many individuals.

A chapter of this book is devoted to my return home from active duty. It was quite literally in the course of piecing together this chapter that I discovered my feelings about coming back were much more pronounced than was expected. These sentiments became increasingly apparent in accordance with the realization of how many obstacles had emerged which prevented me from setting my private practice back on a viable heading. The frustration encountered with this feeling of being set adrift from the financial security of the Army, conjoined with the unresolved feelings about the war and my work in Germany, set the tone for a troubled first year home. The chapter highlights the level of distress I was subjected to, and in so doing, provided a connecting link to the many soldiers returning under somewhat similar psychological conditions.

At the beginning of the war with Iraq (i.e a year before my involuntary deployment to Germany), I had anticipated that there were going to be tremendous needs from Iraqi citizens that could potentially be addressed by psychologists. So, I made an inquiry via e-mail to an Army officer and ranking member of the Military Psychology Division of the American Psychological Association. It read, *"Sir, I am a clinical psychologist in private practice, as well as being an IMA Army Reservist – also as a clinical psychologist.*

As the war in Iraq has progressed, the mental health condition of Iraqi citizens has increasingly been on my mind. Undoubtedly, the Army has sent over sufficient psychologist types to cover for our soldiers in the theatre of operations. But, Sir, my hunch is that the U.S. military may not be prepared to deal with the medical and mental health services of Iraqis in the period when the war is winding down. The problem with reliance on the ICRC and other Volags is that security issues may create difficulties for these organizations to operate effectively.

My sense, Sir, is that a number of Army Reserve psychologists, like myself, may be an untapped resource with regard to a thorough assessment of mental health needs of Iraqi men, women and children, followed by the establishment of short-term interventions that could address these needs. Conducting valuable quantitative and qualitative research with Iraqi citizens, as well as U.S. military personnel, may be another activity worth pursuing.

Since my original enlistment date in 1973 – having a break in service for 7 years before reenlisting in the Reserves in 1983 – it has been a consistent observation that the personnel resources of the military are expansive enough to facilitate positive changes in other countries they are involved in (i.e. when full activated). This certainly pertains, Sir, to the more non-military projects the Army commits to, as well as the strictly military ones.

In any case, Sir, the U.S. aim of helping to rebuild a more democratic Iraq can be well served, at least in my estimation, by military support of medical and mental health needs of Iraqi citizens (i.e. the future of Iraq). The option of utilizing in-house personnel (i.e. Army Reserve medical and mental health personnel) seems to be one way to intervene more immediately while the dust has not yet settled. This also sends a powerful message to the Iraqi population that the American military really does care on the most human of levels.

So, the reason I wrote to you is because of your affiliation with the 'Military Psychology' Division of the APA, as well as your position as an officer with the Army. In part, I want to check out what things are already happening, or are in the works, regarding the above concerns. In addition, I trust some of the thoughts expressed in this e-mail may be useful in one way or another."

My manner of communication must have been received as rather obscure, or focused on a topic he did not want to discuss for unknown reasons. This officer e-mailed me back a one liner stating, *"I am not sure what you want me to provide you, if anything."*

Even though I was not looking for a mentoring relationship here, I was taken aback by the level of interpersonal aloofness oozing out of this terse response. After a sufficient recovery period, I wrote back in an attempt to clarify the issues. I wrote, *"Sir, I apologize for the apparent lack of clarity in my previous e-mail. Actually, you may be able to provide some assistance in some fairly specific ways. As a new member of the Military Psychology Division of APA, I am obviously in a learning mode regarding the areas of interest and involvement of this division. This is definitely true when it comes to the activities/ interests of the Division vis-à-vis military operations in Iraq.*

It would be helpful, Sir, to know the following: (a) whether the Military Psychology Division will be involved in any way with post-war Iraqis regarding clinical treatment, assessment or research; (b) appropriate ways to be involved in or generate discussion and 'brainstorming' of military issues within the Division – post-war clinical matters with both American soldiers and Iraqi citizens included and finally (c) any channels of communication you might recommend for clinical psychologists in the Reserve component – both military and non-military channels – when it pertains to a dialogue about clinical issues related to a war such as the current one in Iraq.

Ultimately, Sir, the driving force behind this inquiry is my own interest in finding avenues of approach within military circles that could facilitate direct involvement on my part, as well as other Reserve psychologists and medical personnel, in providing clinical/assessment services to Iraqi citizens and U.S. soldiers in post-war Iraq."

There is no way of knowing what this official thought about my response. He simply did not reply, or hopefully never received it due to internet problems. But, what came out of it on a personal note was the commencement of a coherent articulation of concerns being developed regarding the psychological needs of various groups directly impacted by the war.

It also served to lay the foundation of the disenchantment that would eventually reach maturity in my mind – that many aspects of this particular war had not been deemed critical enough to consider in advance, and to be adequately addressed when the multitude of problem areas emerged. The seeds were indeed being planted which would lead to my own existential crisis of being out of step, perhaps at cross purposes with the organization I had been affiliated with for twenty nine years.

I would not like to conclude that the unresponsiveness of the above official with the Military Division, American Psychological Association, indicated a lack of interest or concern in the psychological needs of Iraqis. Yet, as the war has progressed, it has certainly become more evident that psychological needs of Iraqis, and even American soldiers, have not received an adequate level of attention.

Even when I began to write, it was not in my mind that such efforts would lead to a book. At best, it was my idea the writing could be shaped in a manner acceptable for certain journals and periodicals. In fact, I went to strenuous lengths to prepare some of the manuscripts for initial proofing and approval by the military in order to then seek publication from a select periodical or journal. Three of the chapters in this book were originally written for just such a purpose.

One of these, *Diplomatic Efforts in the Middle East (Can Psychologists and Conflict Resolution Specialists Contribute to the Negotiation Process),* successfully made it through the Army screening process while I was active duty in Germany. It was subsequently sent off for consideration with a conflict resolution journal.

The submission of the other two articles (i.e. chapters) occurred following my release from active duty in March 2005. Without the tedious, time consuming, and potentially disapproving approach of the military, it seemed to be that my return to the Reserve ranks would remove a major obstacle to publication. It was not too long before both of these remaining articles were sent off to periodicals or journals where some level of interest in the topic was indicated.

It was the unfortunate realities of periodical publishing which really turned the corner for me. One article eventually got approved for publication after nearly a year of reviews. Another year has come and gone in which promises have been made of publishing once this journal staff is in a position to produce another publication. This past January 2006, this article which focused on the conference I attended in Dubai finally was published.

My second article, *Abu Ghraib: A Psychological Search for How Such Dehumanization of Detainees Could Occur,* seemed to promote the greatest level of emotional response. Those in the Army reviewing this work felt strong enough about its content to withhold their authorization for publication in the civilian sector altogether. Once deactivated from the active Army component, other military sponsored journals rejected it in relatively short order. A couple of editors from other journals called for significant changes, as with the idea of writing more about the personality characteristics of the accused soldiers at Abu Ghraib. Depending on who was critiquing the manuscript, it either proved to be too controversial or not forthcoming enough about ethical deficits within the military system.

It was the third article, *Personal Reflections on War, Death and the Act of Living,* that appeared to hold the most promise. I in fact anticipated that a mainstream periodical publication would find this article compatible with the intellectual interests of their readership. Unfortunately, the periodicals picked were so large and widely read that I never received confirmation the manuscript actually underwent anyone's review. My attempt to publish with a larger journal entry directed primarily at health care providers seemed to "backfire." The net result was that it turned out to work against the goal of having editors review this work in the first place.

These setbacks in publishing separate articles led me to the conclusion it might work better to incorporate the articles into a more comprehensive book. The inherent dilemma remained how such seemingly disparate articles could be included under one book title in a way that cohesion and a central theme could be established.

The answer is really contained in the articles themselves. In psychological language, it could be said the solution remained hidden with my own self. As different as the articles are, there is commonality between them. The articles all deal with aspects of the conflict in Iraq and the Middle East. In addition, all of the articles correspond to experiences I have been exposed to during the war years in one fashion or another. Thus, the bottom line for the inspiration and motivation to produce this book pertains to the many ways in which the war years have impacted me both as a psychologist and as an individual human being.

It is my hope this book with assist each reader in his or her own reflections on the war, and the underlying values which are at stake. Also, as often occurs in educational settings, I trust the varied selections herein will provoke many thoughtful questions about our common humanity on this planet - how to coexist with varying beliefs and practices without resorting to military actions that inevitably brings so much human suffering and heartache. Even if liberty and a more secure future are the prizes being sought, the price of those caught in the fray is undeniably enormous. If this book can serve to prompt some individuals toward a quest for alternatives to the unleashing of American power whenever security threats arise, then the time taken to produce this book is not in vein.

Finally, it is my hope this book may by found useful for the many men and woman who are in the armed forces today, many whom have been involved in Operation Iraqi Freedom in one form or another. I trust it will give pause in contemplating who we are as a people, and the principles which we strive to exercise in any setting we find ourselves. It is also my hope the book will encourage individuals to assess the important things which should be asked of our leaders, as they have been designated to carry forward our shared values of individual liberty, freedom of speech, rule of law, humane treatment toward friends and adversaries, and a democratic way of life. These things are worth fighting for - perhaps at great personal risk - and even if accomplished not by the bullet but by the persuasiveness of our words.

References
Brinkley, D. (2004). <u>Tour of duty: John Kerry and the Vietnam war.</u> New York, N.Y.: HarperCollins Publishers.

Fallows, J. (2006). <u>Blind into Baghdad: Americas's war in Iraq.</u> New York, N.Y.:Vantage Books.

CHAPTER 2
DIPLOMATIC EFFORTS
IN THE MIDDLE EAST

Can Psychologists and Conflict Resolutions
Specialists Contribute to the Negotiation Process
(First Published: Online Journal of Peace and
Conflict Resolution, Feb 2006)

There are a variety of ways that a clinical psychologist can write about a particular issue or subject matter. Perhaps the more traditional route involves some form of objectified research and analysis. As much as I might like to utilize such an approach, the actual implementation of this kind of format seems to elude me. So, I have given way to the more precarious mode of communication that is both personal and experiential.

Perhaps it should be noted from the outset that the core theme here is particularly devoted to the "conflictive flash-points" in the Middle East, and the outside powers which have inextricably been drawn to the region as of late. Like so many Americans and citizens of many other countries in the world, the unfolding events in the aftermath of September 11, 2001 have captured my attention enormously, both from a professional and personal standpoint.

The U.S. deployment of troops to Afghanistan initially, and subsequently to Iraq, has profoundly engaged my thoughts and sentiments like few other prolonged situations have ever done. The impact has been particularly dramatic since I am also a clinical psychologist in the Army Reserve. But, as much as my adrenal glands were ignited in anticipation of being activated "down range," it turned out my number remained dormant, leastwise throughout the first year of the war.

What has persistently gnawed on my senses throughout the whole ordeal has been the question of whether the research and clinical sides of psychological practice, as well as those trained in conflict resolution, can have any substantial contribution to make to the current situation that exists in the Middle East today. Despite the possibility psychological analysis and clinical "know how" will be relegated to "arm chair theorizing," I find myself considering the notion again that psychology may have much to offer to the current conflict in Iraq, Israel, and the Middle East as a whole, particularly when various "avenues of approach" are made available.

On a much smaller scale, I am reminded of a psychiatric hospital I have been affiliated with. There have been several departmental turf battles, interpersonal conflicts, longstanding resentments, managerial disregard for adequate staffing, and what can be considered a widespread state of staff apathy and burnout. These problems have been noted for years, despite the presence of psychologists with considerable skills in conflict resolution, effective team building, and management-employee problem solving strategies.

One key obstacle preventing behavioral health professionals from having a positive impact is that they have rarely been given a "green light" from management to address these issues. So, whether the setting is in a psychiatric hospital, for instance, or in an international context, the knowledge and skills psychologists possess regarding human behavior are likely to have greater difficulties being realized when a viable role has not been designated for them.

My difficulty since 911 has been to find opportunities where psychologists and conflict resolution professionals can effectively exercise the "tools of their trade" in such a way that their expertise and proposed interventions actually impact the decisions of policy makers in the United States, other countries in the Middle East, and many other countries associated with the events in the Middle East.

During the initial stages of Operation Iraqi Freedom, I attended a local Rotary Club meeting where a retired three star General gave a presentation on military steps being employed in the Iraqi theatre of operations. He responded cordially to a question posed regarding how much thought military leaders had given to addressing the prospect of another generation of terrorists emerging in years to come. His response was to note the armed forces were still operating in a reactive mode. It was therefore his assessment the military by and large had not yet been able to seriously evaluate the psychological forces at work which might lead to another wave of fresh terrorists "down the road" (i.e. terrorists "in the wings," so to speak).

As understandable as it is that the primary focus of the military has been directed toward a decisive defeat of terrorist objectives, the simultaneous focus on the "larger landscape" is one particularly well suited to psychologists. Many social scientists, psychologists, psychiatrists, social workers, and those trained in conflict resolution, have much to contribute to a deeper understanding of current terrorist mentality, the necessary ingredients needed to perpetuate more terrorism in the years to come, and conversely approaches likely to diminish future terrorist recruits (Cassimatis, 2002; Moghaddam & Marsella, eds., 2004; Silke, 2003; Social Affairs Data-Mining, 2002).

In December 2003, an opportunity for psychologists emerged with regard to events in the Middle East. The very first Middle East/North Africa Regional Conference in Psychology convened for close to a week in Dubai, United Arab Emirates (UAE). This conference was largely attended by psychologists and other mental health providers from various countries in the Gulf region and the Middle East as a whole, as well as a few from assorted distant countries. I was one of a small handful of American participants at the conference. Even though Israelis would not normally be allowed into an Arab county like the UAE, arrangements were made for several psychologists/academicians from Israel to bypass the normal entry point through Customs and be present for the conference.

A stated purpose of the conference was to address what impact Psychology could have on the various conflicts in the region. However, given the scientific nature of the conference, the focus was predominantly directed to research-based presentations. Some exceptions did occur, such as a presentation by a Palestinean therapist describing her work with Palestinean women traumatized by the death of their spouses in Israel. However, very little attention was given to the current problem of American soldiers engaged in armed conflict within two Arab countries, and how psychologists might help to ameliorate the extent of the conflict and the rising death toll for indigenous Afghanis, Iraqis, American soldiers, other Coalition forces, and contract workers alike.

I also received approval to conduct an impromptu Networking session to facilitate ongoing connections following the conclusion of the conference. This at least allowed a forum for me to inform the group of nine participants my interest in the roles psychologists might have regarding peacemaking in the region. My proposed area of interest did not spawn the kind of dialogue I had hoped for. Many factors very likely accounted for this lack of enthusiastic feedback – two reasons possibly being my "outsider" status and their view of the intractable nature of these regional conflicts.

My exposure to a more Arab approach to the field of psychology through my involvement at this conference did prove to be useful, even regarding the question I was attempting to find an answer to. For one thing, a dominant theme of the conference impressed itself on me – this being a profound distrust Arab practitioners appeared to have toward a westernized form of psychology being imposed on them. As has increasingly come to the fore with many cultural and ethnic groups, a number of participants were noting that the Arab world deeply steeped in Islamic values had need of developing their own culture-specific psychology.

This suggested to me that any viable peacemaking and conflict resolution strategies would likely be enhanced by incorporating an Arab/Islamic world view. Otherwise, any conflict resolution approaches employed by psychologists would easily be considered irrelevant, or at least flawed, in fostering reduced tensions in the region.

All the American-bred optimism in the universality of their democratic principles and psychological understanding of human beings could in the final analysis serve as an obstacle for the peace process in the Middle East. Embarrassing as it is to admit, I too have to acknowledge the inclination of exporting my own understanding of psychological principles onto the Arab world, and of course expecting a positive outcome.

It just so happened my presence at the conference coincided with the capture of Sadam Hussein. The timing was fortuitous beyond the obvious in the sense it enabled me to discover another form of thinking in the Arab world quite different from what I was familiar with in the West. It appeared one reaction amongst some Arabs involved a feeling of ambivalence. While relieved a dictatorial leader was being brought to justice, there seemed to be a concern that even an Arab tyrant should not be publicly humiliated – this being especially the case at the hands of a Western power.

One woman I talked with about it indicated her displeasure that Sadam's extended family, particularly the children, would be subjected to endless replays of Sadam's disheveled and haggard looking countenance – a shaming experience for any Arab family to experience. The importance of preserving family honor struck me as a critical piece of effective work in this area of the world, and one which so unwittingly from a western mindset could be violated.

As much as the conference expanded my horizons as a psychologist with international interests, and an American one at that, the lingering question remains in force. It is a much tougher arena for psychologists to function in, this being the diplomatic front, than the more familiar terrain of clinical work and research/teaching. It may be the formal invitations some of us keep awaiting may be long in materializing, just as has been the case with the psychiatric hospital referred to earlier.

That some pioneering psychologists and conflict resolution professionals have found workable avenues from which to operate as effective peacemakers (Aoki, 2000; Hanlon, 2003; Kelman, 2000; Salzinger, 2003; Sleek, 1998) says a lot about their tenacity to "stay the course," even when the progress made may occur on the fringes of thorny "flashpoints" that career diplomats/politicians, government officials and military leaders find so problematic in forging out agreements, deals, cease fires, and diminishment of conflicts.

Still, it is worth noting the research work for this article did not yield any evidence that psychologists and conflict resolution specialists had ever participated directly in the Arab-Israeli negotiations. This absence of involvement was additionally maintained by two presenters of Palestinean-Israeli issues at the International Conference of Political Psychology in July 2004.

This article could not go to "press" quickly enough before my involvement with Middle Eastern affairs would take another unexpected and divergent turn. The Army did in fact decide to call me up for military duty. Rather than to the "sandbox," as military personnel often refer to the Middle East, my assignment was to Landstuhl, Germany. The need for psychologists assigned to the outpatient psychiatric wing of the regional hospital had increased. This was due in part to the growing volume of soldiers who came in from Afghanistan and Iraq – Landstuhl being used as a kind of weigh station before soldiers moved on to the U.S. or back to their original unit "down range."

My clinical skills were tested in new ways, such as evaluations conducted by me pertaining to the mental health stability of soldiers pulled from varied operational areas in the Middle East. Determinations had to be made whether such soldiers could return to their units in the Middle East and once again be considered viable team members.

There were also the family members left behind in Germany who struggled in various ways with being separated and uncertain about the future. My schedule two days a week, and subsequently expanded to three days a week, placed me at the Family Health Clinic, Baumholder Army Post where large components of the 1st Armored Division had been deployed to Iraq for a year originally, and then an additional extension for up to 120 days. My caseload there had been primarily comprised of spouses dealing with the stresses of being apart from their "soldier spouse," their own mental-emotional struggles, and managing their children alone over this extended time frame. However with the return of most of the Brigade from Iraq in July 2004, I worked more with soldiers adjusting to the very different demands of military life in the "rear."

The reality of the escalation of tension in Iraq impacted me on two fronts. One front was the steady barrage of media highlighting the mounting drama with religious/political groups such as the Shiites and Sunnis, along with other "flashpoints" like Baghdad, Fallujah, and the January 2005 elections. The other front involved the soldiers themselves landing on the "Landstuhl doorstep," often with little more than the rumpled uniform they wore during the initial days back and a rather bewildered and lost look in their eyes.

Again the haunting question came back to me in the midst of my daily clinical work with soldiers and family members. It pressed upon me even more pointedly as U.S. soldiers contended with an escalation of insurgent violence against many different individuals and groups considered to be cooperating with the U.S. This personal inquiry seemed to burn in my mind as again the world watched, military and civilian alike, with anticipation and dread that the level of violence and instability in future months could escalate to more tragic proportions. And yes, the Army hospital here in Landstuhl had learned to anticipate heightened trauma - medical and mental health staff alike - soberly prepared for those episodes of an increased volume of physically and mentally compromised soldiers flooding in from "down range."

Is it possible properly trained psychologists and conflict resolution professionals really could positively impact the outcome of conflicts as primed for protracted bloodletting as with Iraq and the Israeli-Palestinean struggle? The best that can be done thus far, it would seem, is to pose the hypothesis with the hope that greater levels of applied research might occur. It can further be hypothesized the area of negotiations most compatible with the training and skills of clinical psychologists and conflict resolution specialists pertains to the "process work" of the talks as opposed to the content domain.

Of course, in order to secure the most meaningful research on this question, psychologists and conflict resolution professionals would need to be brought into the arena as genuine contributors where actual negotiations and decisions are made - ones determining the course the differing sides will take in a conflict. Arriving at this point does not have to be in the distant future, as there remains time for such experimentation even germane to the current conflict in Iraq between the American military, the terrorist groupings, disillusioned Iraqis, factional religious groups, and outside Arab entities.

I have gone through graduate school and practiced as a psychologist during a time when the horizons for psychologically related endeavors has dramatically expanded. This implies a growing recognition that practitioners of psychological principles can positively benefit human enterprises across the spectrum, even with regard to international conflicts and wars.

The American Psychological Association (APA), as noted by Crawford (2003), has highlighted this potential with what is termed "peace psychologists," recognizing a need for standardizing this area of practice to insure adequate training and expertise. It may be the time is nearing when one of the oldest dilemmas known to humankind – this being intractable conflicts culminating in much bloodshed – will become accessible to the strange, but penetrating tools of psychologists and conflict resolution specialists who regularly practice the art of negotiation, compromise, and identifying with the merits of both sides within the confines of private offices, conference rooms and the like.

References

Aoki, C. (2000). Many cultures at work: Psychological scientists in the private sector.
American Psychological Association:
News and Research, 13(9).

APA Press Releases. (2002, November 19). Social science data-mining and decision tree analysis techniques are important to anti-terrorism programs. Retrieved June 27, 2004, from http:/www.apa.org/releases/apa_fbi.html

Cassimatis, E.G. (2002). Terrorism, our world and our way of life. Journal of American Academy of Psychoanalysis, 0(4), 531-543.

Crawford, N. (2003). Social responsibility during conflict and war: Peace psychologists re-examine ethics and best practices in the world's conflict zones. APA Monitor, 34(6), 30-32.

Hanlon, P. (2004). Psychologists hope to make an impact. Mass Psy.com, 12(1).

Kelman, H. C. (2000). The role for the scholar-practitioner in international conflict resolution.
International Studies Perspective, 1(3), 273-287.

Moghaddam, F. M. and Marsella, A. J. (Eds.), (2004). Understanding terrorism: Psychosocial roots, consequences, and interventions. Washington D.C.: American Psychological Association.

Salzinger, K. (2003). War zone: Learning from social psychology: Social psychologist Herbert Kelman discusses Middle East peace process. <u>Psychology Today</u>, May/Jun.

Silke, A. (2003). Beyond horror: Terrorist atrocity and the search for understanding – The case of the Shankill bombing. <u>Studies in Conflict and Terrorism</u>, 26(1), 37-60.

Sleek, S. (1998). Quelling ethnopolitical strife is the goal of new initiative: A new Center will train a cadre of scientist-practitioners who specialize in easing conflict between ethnic or political groups, <u>APA Monitor</u>, 29(3).

CHAPTER 3
PERSONAL REFLECTIONS ON WAR, DEATH AND THE ACT OF LIVING

Through the Work of a Psychologist with American Soldiers at Landstuhl and Baumholder, Germany During Operation Iraqi Freedom

Whether one has fear of it or not, one's death is difficult to accept. Sordo had accepted it but there was no sweetness in its acceptance even at fifty two, with three wounds and surrounded on a hill…If one must die, he thought, and clearly one must, I can die. But I hate it. Dying was nothing and he had no picture of it nor fear of it in his mind. But living was a field of grain blowing in the wind on the side of a hill. Living was a hawk in the sky. Living was an earthen jar of water in the dust of the threshing with the grain flailed out and the chaff blowing. Living was a horse between your legs and a carbine under one leg and a hill and a valley and a stream with trees along it and the far side of the valley and the hills beyond (Hemmingway, 1940, p. 191).

At the beginning of "Operation Iraqi Freedom" I volunteered for deployment, feeling my skills as a Reserve clinical psychologist could be well utilized for American soldiers and the Iraqi citizenry we wanted to help. But, it goes deeper than that, as things usually do. My reason for originally joining the Army in 1973 was based on a sense of obligation to do my part in the Vietnam conflict. Yet, the timing was off, as a peace agreement between the United States and Vietnam was formed just at the time of my enlistment. One way or another, these early efforts to undergo firsthand the rigors of combat eluded me.

Within a year of my initial enlistment, the Captain I worked for informed me that the entire 82nd Airborne Division was going into a combat zone. Even back then, events in the Middle East were shaping the future of American soldiers. We were bused down to the adjoining Air Force base where we sat on the runway for hours, all suited up with those cinched up parachutes. At the final hour, rapid deployment was terminated. We were told the Russians had decided not to risk a showdown with the United States, instead allowing the Arabs and Israelis to fight out the Third Arab-Israeli War on their own. So rather than jumping into the Middle Eastern desert with weapons loaded, we were able to put away our chutes and resume normal garrison life at Fort Bragg, N.C.

During this three year stint (i.e. 1973-76), I was subsequently assigned to the northernmost unit in South Korea before reaching the demilitarized zone. It was well understood that if North Korea ever did carry out a pre-emptive invasion of South Korea, our little mechanized infantry battalion would be overrun and liquidated within hours. Their big guns were sighted in on us just across the border. Obviously, the anticipated moment of dread remained only that during my time there. I completed my tour and returned home for a much desired discharge.

Somehow the lure of military life drew me back to the Army Reserve in 1983, quite to my surprise. Previously, I thought I had permanently put it behind me. Several quiet years went by in the Reserve before I confronted once again the possibility of being involved in a war zone. Working then as an Intelligence Analyst, I was asked to help support the soldiers in Panama in the aftermath of the overthrow of Noriega (i.e. 1989). This was really my first trip into an area that had just undergone combat operations. The sight of ransacked offices and bombed out buildings was a new experience for me.

The reality of being in a combat zone hit me the moment I stepped off the military transport. Wearing full combat gear, we were ushered to a pick-up point in the dark. This left me with the ominous sense that our safety was more precarious in this environment. Thankfully, no incidents occurred in those 30 days I was there. Probably the most apprehensive I was about being shot was when I jogged at night through some darkened streets inside our compound. Several times, I imagined the prospects of infiltrators sneaking across the fence to lie in wait of a hapless runner like myself. My level of hyper-vigilance thus remained elevated to where I noticed every unusually shaped shadow and the array of night noises in the jungle-like bush.

This collection of past experiences in the military had a cumulative effect in a recurrent dream that surfaced occasionally, although presented in a number of varying scenarios. Still the theme remained, one involving preparations for battle which often included the frightening feelings of being on the verge of engaging the enemy in a ferocious conflagration. The other sub-theme of these dreams highlighted myself in a personal state of poor readiness while all the other soldiers were performing adequately. Although, these normally did not startle or awaken me, the vivid details did impact me on many occasions with unsettled thoughts.

I have not been one to dwell much on the topic of death. I have never found it a particularly intriguing topic, even when talking to clients about their issues and concerns with death.

As with most of us, there are reasons for the way our mind avoids certain topics. My discomfort with death most likely goes back to a car accident when I was twelve. Our whole family was in the car at the time it lost control and veered into oncoming traffic at 70 miles per hour. Although I had been sleeping in the front seat, the vague memory of the event suggests I woke up and watched us lurch across the grassy divider. Everyone was hospitalized from the injuries we sustained. My Dad took the brunt of the impact on the passenger side of the front seat, and he died within a week from kidney failure. As hard as it was to grapple with his death, it was additionally difficult to deal with the funeral process and the "mourning family" protocols we were expected to carry out. The adverse affect compelled me to avoid other funerals, and my father's gravesite, for years to come.

The events of 911 had a tremendous impact on me. This occurred the first day of my new Army assignment to the Behavioral Clinic at Ft. Polk, Louisiana. Up to this point in the Army, I had been a Reserve sergeant who had worked as an intelligence analyst. Now, upon the very commencement of this new career path as an Army Reserve clinical psychologist, my first hours on the job were spent in a surreal fog with other staff members attempting to embrace the sheer magnitude of this national tragedy. Grasping the full meaning and far reaching impact of the event was something which took several days, perhaps weeks, for me to realize.

This highly coordinated attack on American soil, and the many lives lost in a matter of minutes, brought me in touch with the utter fragility of life. The idea that typical people carrying out a normal day at work could suddenly be thrust into life and death situations etched a deep furrow in my mind, some of which I probably was incapable as yet of fully comprehending on a conscious level.

Some two years after 911, I encountered the worst form of dread I can remember in adulthood about my own eventual death and termination of existence. The occasion was a trip in December 2003 to a psychology conference in Dubai, United Arab Emirates. Certainly there was some concern about my reception there as an American in an Arab country at a time when sentiments toward Americans were seemingly negative. In honesty, a pervasive sense of doom cast its shadow over me while flying over the Atlantic Ocean. I imagined the airplane barely suspended in the sky by a thin thread which at any time would be severed, sending the plane plummeting to the earth's surface, and bursting into thousands of fiery pieces upon impact with the ocean. And, at this precise moment - just seconds before having experienced a heightened awareness and sickening dread - my earthly existence would cease. The horrific thought of this contingency was unbearable, and waiting for the potentiality seemed more horrendous than experiencing it outright

I could fully appreciate the celebrated Russian author, Dostoevsky, who stood before a firing squad and, fully horrified, awaited the firing of the bullet which would instantaneously terminate his life – he receiving a reprieve in the final seconds before the rifles were fired.

In keeping with Dostoevsky's fright, my plane obviously did not fall out of the sky, although it could have, and I endured this existential crisis. But the issues of life and death did not recede into the background for long. Once again, the Army set the stage for an unexpected turn of events which would challenge my thinking about life and death anew.

Just as I had accepted the reality of not being called up by the Army, the phone message arrived in February 2004 that I was being deployed to Germany for a year. My assignment would be to work as a psychologist in Outpatient Psychiatry at Landstuhl Regional Medical Center. Within a thirty day period, my private practice was closed, and as many business and personal issues as possible had been handled. My fiancé even assumed "power of attorney" to manage my affairs.

Naturally, there were endless uncertainties about my new assignment. One very prominent uncertainty was whether this initial assignment in Germany would culminate in being sent to Iraq. My new boss assured me this would not happen, as I was truly needed at Landstuhl. My sentiments about a possible deployment to Iraq were mixed. The day to day living conditions did not sound very inviting – long hours, intolerable heat, and sand everywhere. Not surprisingly, the prospect of being maimed or killed there also served as a damper.

But, as mentioned earlier, a counterweight to these misgivings lured me toward a kind of perverse hope that I, too, would be selected. Then, at last, I would learn how well I could hold up under a stressful existence in combat conditions. The waiting and wondering would then have been resolved.

The cards, however, did not get dealt that way. Instead, my role was relegated to that of a psychologist providing clinical services in the rear, close to the combat theatre only from an emotional standpoint. This scenario gave considerable comfort, knowing that my fiancé and children were much relieved. Still, sometimes more than others, I would struggle with feelings of "getting off easy," not being a "true" soldier, and ultimately still not having fully confronted my existential issues. Even at age fifty, it seemed I needed to prove myself under the most extreme conditions – like a return to those early football practices when full contact seemed so scary and unnerving.

The chief psychiatrist and my boss, a neuro-psychologist, formulated a plan for how I would be best utilized. They decided that the greatest need was for a therapist to conduct ongoing therapy to patients. The permanent psychiatrists and psychologists had been focused on doing assessments, psychological testing, and prescribing of medications. This left me available for assignments at the outpatient psychiatry wing at the hospital two times a week, and to another post, Baumholder, three days a week. So, by the beginning of April, I began developing two separate caseloads for the two sites. At Baumholder, I became the sole psychologist for predominantly spouses of soldiers from the 1st Armored Division, whose soldiers had been in Iraq for the past year.

In addition to conducting therapy for individual patients at the hospital, I also saw soldiers returning from Iraq and Afghanistan who had been identified with mental health difficulties. My challenging task was to assess whether a given soldier was fit to return to his unit as a viable member, or be required evacuation to the States for further care. Conducting these interviews was often difficult, especially when a soldier wanted to return to Iraq while psychological symptoms persisted. There was something rather unsettling about making such weighty decisions from a single session or two.

These soldiers brought back considerable "inside" information about the war in Iraq. Vicariously, I was living out many of these experiences through the often graphic descriptions they provided. The degree of combat exposure varied tremendously from one soldier to the next. But, even if a soldier had not shot at (or been shot at by) the enemy, and had not witnessed friendly or enemy forces being killed, most had experienced potentially threatening events.

The most frequently reported event involved the utterly helpless feeling during a mortar attack. A typical attack of this kind was reported to be most likely during the night sometime after soldiers had "hit the rack." As the mortars pounded in, soldiers would fly about in an attempt to dawn all their gear, including flak jackets, for their protection. Although most of the mortars would hit areas of the compound where soldiers were scarce, others would strike extremely close to groups of soldiers, causing injuries and sometimes fatalities. An early direct hit could literally kill some soldiers before they ever made it out of bed. So unsettling was this experience that going out on patrols in the streets, or going on house raids, was actually preferred to the mortar attacks. There seemed to be a pervasive feeling of being like a "sitting duck" which at any unexpected moment could be one's last. Even with the roadside "IED's" (i.e. improvised explosive devices), soldiers often reported feeling more comfort, as they could at least visually scan for possible bombs along the roadway, and thereby be more in control of their situation.

Prompted by these accounts, I have found myself wondering on many occasions what it would feel like to be in this kind of environment. It seemed almost unimaginable to fully grasp the reality that one's very life hovered so close to death's door, regardless of whether or not one put on all the gear or continued to lie on one's bed. There literally was not any safe corner to run for protection. Call it a matter of chance, or call it divinely ordained providence, there was no predicting when or where those mortars would land. One episode would seem traumatic enough, but to endure it night after night – losing sleep over it – might possibly push the psyche to its breaking point.

I needed to make on the spot decisions either to return a soldier into this kind of hellish situation, or to send them home out of harm's way. As I would later find out from other practitioners, very few soldiers were sent back "downrange" after making it to our unit at Landstuhl. Even for those committed soldiers who wanted to go back to do their part for the unit, evacuation to Landstuhl often made for low motivation to return. The stark contrast between the austere environment of Iraq to the plush greenery of Germany was so pronounced that it facilitated internal resistance for deployment to Baghdad a second time.

My introduction to the Baumholder Health Clinic came almost simultaneously to when the military decided to extend all of the First Armored Division. This occurred at a time when the fighting in Iraq had escalated. This event seemed to have a marked impact on many of the spouses at Baumholder. I was certainly doing considerable therapy with select spouses who were struggling with the extension. A number of the spouses I worked with felt this extension was a very hard reality to accept, reminding them that they could not place too much trust in given Army plans, as things are frequently in fluctuation.

Following these early experiences at Baumholder, a seminal event occurred which really heightened for me the painful reality of war. A car bomb had killed 8 soldiers, all of them from Baumholder. This had a devastating affect on the entire Baumholder community. It proved to be doubly destabilizing, given that these soldiers would all still be alive if they had only returned home as originally planned.

A memorial service was held in the chapel. The helmets and boots of the 8 soldiers were visible to all attending by being prominently situated on a podium. It occurred to me during the service that I was now being called upon to exercise my clinical skills in new and very challenging ways. This incident, and my attendance at the memorial, was making it much more difficult to maintain the necessary professional distance. I now was being thrust headlong into an arena where I needed to find ways to deal with patients impacted by these deaths, all while grappling with my own internal uneasiness about death and dying issues. How could I provide beneficial therapeutic approaches when so many of my own inner tensions regarding death were proliferating?

Many of the spouses came to see me during this extension period. My appointment schedule continued to remain booked out for a week to two weeks. They often needed a safe place in which to vent their frustration, anger, and overwhelming sadness. Fears of their loved ones also being killed or wounded were quite prominent with most of the spouses, whether or not they were overtly expressed. Some of these women were involved in the Family Readiness Group which served as a support network for spouses at Baumholder. They were keenly aware of their friends who had received the fateful visit by a flag-bearing soldier in dress uniform. It proved to be a very significant challenge for many spouses to carry on their normal daily functions, to include even the care for their children.

As a practitioner, it was hard for me to sort out genuine psychological difficulties when the spouses at Baumholder were all subjected to very stressful circumstances. Each of them had to find their own way of coping and carrying on with life. In many cases, spouses came to my office with pronounced adjustment problems directly related to the deployment. Conversely, a number of spouses reported struggles which appeared quite independent from deployment issues.

Raising children as a "single parent" was a common complaint expressed. They were now having to provide comfort for their children in dealing with the absence of a parent and the uncertainty of the outcome – coupled with the daily oversight of their children's schooling, activities, discipline, and overall needs. As anticipated, the return of the soldiers brought to a close my clinical work with a sizeable number of spouses who had faithfully attended sessions previously. I can only surmise that the reunion diminished the psychological symptoms to a manageable level for many of them.

Alternatively, there were spouses who were not looking forward to the return of their soldier, due to problems that had surfaced either prior to, or during, the deployment period. I worked with some who did not want to upset their spouses downrange because it seemed like bad timing to separate and divorce. For a few then, the extension was welcomed, as it allowed more time of tranquility and independence. The extension also allowed more unhindered time for some spouses to continue extramarital relationships with "closet partners."

July proved to be the redeeming month. The entire Armored Brigade had been notified that they would leave Iraq for Germany at varying times throughout the month. A whole cadre of soldiers in the rear were tasked to help with a recently structured 7-day reintegration period. This would be accomplished with the use of several tents set up for the reintegration alone. Each of the seven days involved movement to the different stations where necessary information for the reintegration was provided. Those of us covering for "mental health' screens were involved in day three (3) only. The physicians saw these soldiers first, and then referred some for mental health assessments. It was estimated that roughly ten percent of the soldiers going through reintegration would actually receive a mental health screening.

For the first time in the war, I met with a cross section of soldiers who had remained functional in a combat zone, despite some psychological symptoms. These were generally not soldiers the Command had singled out for marked mental health difficulties. It seemed the case that these soldiers had been more silent and covert about any psychological symptoms when compared with the soldiers being evacuated specifically to Landstuhl.

Their common symptoms included sleep disturbances, depression, anxiety, and post traumatic stress. For some, the anxiety had increased with the return to Germany. In fact some whom I met with in the tents had stressors significant enough to warrant a referral for psychiatric hospitalization. They were experiencing major adjustment problems in dealing with the ambiguities of a non-combat environment.

Other soldiers, also including many hospitalized ones, had desired to return to Iraq. Unbelievable as it was from my perspective, they truly felt their lives made more sense in Iraq. There was a lot of structure and daily routines to which they had grown accustomed. Their lives seemed less complicated there. Also, some felt incredibly committed to their units, and believed that their continued involvement would make a difference. A few were convinced their special skills were needed in the ongoing fight against terrorism and the Iraqi insurgency.

In the weeks leading up to the reintegration period, the officer in charge of Behavioral Services at Landstuhl confided that heightened "anger" had been very widespread with soldiers returning from various places in Iraq. This analysis confirmed my observation, at least from the soldiers I screened in the tents. A lot of frustration fomented "downrange," some towards faceless enemy insurgents responsible for IED's, suicide car bombings, mortar and rocket attacks, and checkpoint killings. The environmental conditions (i.e. heat, long hours, and sand storms) just added to the sentiments of being helpless against both human and natural forces.

Several of the soldiers I screened were quite verbose about their frustrations with the Iraqi people. They often noted that the American soldiers' sense of goodwill toward Iraqis had been lessened by the increased loss of American lives – even occurring at times in proximity of Iraqi crowds. When incidents did occur, the crowds reportedly would not disperse easily. Much to the chagrin of the soldiers, the throngs of curious bystanders would actually press forward to get a closer look. A number of the soldiers I talked with thus referred to Iraqis in derogatory ways, seeing them as "stupid and irrational, and very irritating." These perceived differences seemed to help cement prejudicial beliefs.

The range of combat experiences in Iraq varied greatly. Some soldiers reported never even needing to discharge their weapons on the enemy the entire time in Iraq. Similarly, some had never witnessed any actual killings of enemy or friendly forces, nor seen any friendly or enemy dead bodies in the streets or in buildings. For some, the entire time in Iraq was anesthetized from any real traumatic incidents.

For others, particularly the lower ranking enlisted soldiers, their experiences involved frequent direct contact with enemy fire, friendly and enemy killings, and sights of dead bodies. Soldiers in this category often performed the more harrowing jobs of urban patrols, house raids, convoys and security at checkpoints. These tasks put them at greater risk of being ambushed, shot at by small arms, rocket or mortar attacks, or subjected to car bombs and IED's.

The level of cohesion reportedly was a key factor for how well some soldiers dealt with their time in Iraq. Even when the unit as a whole was struggling with interpersonal challenges and poor morale, having some close ties with a small network of "battle buddies" seemed to make a difference. Those operating more as "loners" either of choice or of having been ostracized, often reported marked difficulties that impacted their overall emotional stability. Some soldiers noted the social difficulties as being so problematic that these issues overshadowed the normal concerns of being in a combat zone.

It has perplexed me on several occasions in learning about soldiers suffering from psychological difficulties, often in conjunction with interpersonal issues, and that their removal from the theatre of operations and referral to behavioral health seemed to occur in an inconsistent, almost case-by-case manner. In some instances steps were taken almost immediately to send a soldier back to Germany for further assessment. However, there were other cases when soldiers were retained in their units for lengthy periods, at times including restrictions, discipline, and humiliation. One soldier with both mental health and substance abuse problems admitted he had assumed the "black sheep" role within his unit.

I am intrigued that such interpersonal tensions and conflicts, even being scapegoated, has such a central role in the same arena where soldiers are facing dangerous encounters with the insurgents almost daily. Perhaps it could be argued that these relational problems are the outgrowth of the unique kinds of stresses, irritations, and frustrations soldiers experience in combat. These kind of dynamics may also serve the purpose of providing some vent for latent anxieties related to the war.

Following the return of many soldiers from block leave in August, I noted an increase of appointments. Some of these individuals had experienced a pronounced increase in anxiety, depression and post traumatic stress symptoms. These soldiers had typically never had any prior treatment of any kind. They have confirmed my observation that their reluctance to seek out treatment in a military environment can be overcome when debilitating symptoms come on the horizon that compromise self-reliance.

Soldiers commonly reported a heightened state of fear, and sometimes dread, upon their initial entry into Iraq. Yet, most of them have implied that this eventually waned. Amazingly, they adapt to existing in a hostile environment where disaster, even death, loomed continually. Of course, most humans learn to adapt to their environment, as opposed to contemplating regularly that, for example, one's next car ride may result in a fatal accident. Yet, the knowledge that an enemy is very invested in killing American soldiers and Iraqi civilians creates a higher state of danger that westernized civilizations do not experience. That soldiers are able to normalize their daily existence to such an extent that these harsh realities are actually managed truly implies a level of human resiliency that most of us will not be called upon to confront.

Perhaps what I have witnessed from my exposure to the lives of many returning soldiers is an amazing amount of fortitude. Yet this capacity to meet intense, life threatening adversity has emanated from "common" people from all walks of life who now wear the uniform. Most of these soldiers reached this point through a series of circumstances beyond their control that has placed them directly in harm's way, compelling all of them to strive for ongoing "mental toughness."

Even so, as I have found in my work, a number of soldiers struggled with the demands placed on them in this austere, hot, dreary, extraordinarily miserable environment - one where the specter of human suffering and degradation filled the senses, at times near the breaking point. Reflective of the "civilian world," there are some who were unable to endure the rigors of Iraq similar to "soldiers" in the mainstream, to include those with physical and psychological conditions. Even in the face of daunting complications both physically and psychologically, some of these soldiers were desperate to return to the combat zone and complete their tour of duty. Others more willingly, and gratefully, returned home despite the oft felt shame, knowing that a return to Iraq would very likely destabilize them, and in turn create problems for their unit.

This sense of duty and the need to be regarded favorably by fellow soldiers and family occasionally went counter to thoughts of self-preservation. Some soldiers indicated a preference of returning to Iraq and even being killed, rather than suffer the utter humiliation of removal from combat for psychological reasons.

As I have witnessed, the soldiers, spouses, and families at Baumholder have gone through nearly a year and a half of stress and uncertainty – something akin to what other military communities around the globe have also experienced. They endured the harrowing prospect of prolonged separation that included numerous combat deaths of some of their soldiers, spouses and parents.

This placed the kind of demands on the Baumholder community that cannot be adequately expressed in words. How can one begin to articulate a daily kind of dread and never ending fear - coming from the soldiers, their spouses, and their children – that the temporarily painful separation (albeit lengthy) might result at any moment in a permanent and irreversible rupture? For, even in my office, where often repressed and forbidden feelings and thoughts are allowed the freedom to surface, spouses struggled tremendously to give voice to these horrific contingencies and negative realities. A number of them focused on positive considerations, as with parenting and housekeeping, rather than these feared possibilities.

My involvement within the Baumholder community has thus turned out to be as unique and meaningful as any clinical work I have ever had. Never before have I felt so rightly utilized. The entire Health Clinic, including several of the physicians, utilized me in a most needed manner. It struck me that the entire community was absolutely surging with fundamental psychological needs that many within their ranks had recognized. Quite honestly, I did not fully know how to respond to their neediness, nor my status as such a highly valued commodity. Not only were physicians making many referrals to me, but they were literally walking patients into my office and soliciting my thoughts about medications. The stress amongst health care providers and staff was likewise acutely apparent, as both staff members and family members were coming to me for therapy as well.

While not to wax Messianic, I liken the experience to outstretched hands passing me from person to person in a thronging sea of human need. The typical guard against psychological issues seemed to be minimal, as staff and patients were virtually transparent in their recognition of the struggles facing many within this community. It is as if the strain of the war in Iraq has demonstrated how appropriate it is to admit we all have eventual limits in coping ability.

Final Thoughts Before Departure From Germany - Jan. 2005

My time at Baumholder and at Landstuhl Regional Medical Center will soon end. My plan is to return to civilian life and a normal Reserve status by early March 2005. My direct exposure to combat will likely elude me, as it has during other conflicts at earlier points in my military career. My question will remain with regard to how I would have handled the threat of insurgent attacks and combat life. I will return home still lacking the "hands on" lesson(s) of war and all the psychological impulses that get activated. I will still only be able to relate to war second hand, and the threat of instantaneous annihilation will remain only an intellectual abstraction that will ebb and flow within my mind.

But it is now easier to accept my fate of staying out of Iraq in spite of the noblest notions of being there and performing my duties admirably. The soldiers at Baumholder and at Landstuhl have provided me an abundance of information about the experience of being down range and what it was like for them. Not much of it sounded the least inviting, espe-

cially when referring back to past discussions with veterans, readings of war, and what my mind can fathom vicariously about the reality of friendly & enemy forces and civilians being maimed or killed. My lack of direct exposure to war is not a bad thing, and is preferable to the inner trauma often ushered in by the unnatural state of armed conflict. The vast majority of soldiers I have spoken with from Baumholder and Landstuhl certainly offer some compelling reasons for not relishing the prospect of gaining combat experience.

My Baumholder experience in particular encourages me that what I have done here is sufficient and needed. It has emphasized that, even amongst soldiers risking their lives in combat, life remains the preferred option. Many of the soldiers I have met have reminded me that however close the jaws of death have come, we crave for life and a return to normalcy beyond the chaos, uncertainty, and horrors experienced in combat or life in general.

Certainly, my struggle with the inevitability of death has been impacted by my work here in Germany, and especially so in Baumholder. My work with spouses and soldiers brought me closer to the shared dilemma with which we all grapple. It emphasized for me the amount of inner courage individuals are capable of mustering in accepting their own mortality and those they love most dearly.

Whether spoken, or felt, the Baumholder community was compelled to go several steps ahead of many of the rest of us in embracing just how closely death hovers over all our lives. But, along with this sobering recognition, the longing for a momentary reprieve from death becomes all the more tenacious and all the more valued. The idea of having their spouses back to once again hold hands, go for a walk, and to simply be close to a person they love was all that was sought. All the other considerations of family life mattered as well, but there seemed in many instances a greater level of aware-ness of the intrinsic need for merely being in the presence of their spouse and the object of their love. One soldier return-ing from Iraq noted that he feared far less the loss of his own life in comparison with the dreaded prospect of not seeing his spouse and child one more time.

Now at age fifty, still amazed about what happened during my last thirty years, it has not been easy to recognize and face the finiteness of my life. In some way, the encounters I have shared with spouses and soldiers at Landstuhl, and Baum-holder especially, have strengthened me to respond more courageously than I previously thought possible to my own decline. And, more importantly for the unknown remainder of my life, it has served to illuminate what things about living are truly essential and of infinite value, and therefore worthy of my utmost attention – my fiancé, children, family of origin, friends, professional pursuits, and other worthy projects that enhance the human enterprise of living and fulfillment. Re-turning home instead of down range will provide the context where these ends can be served most profoundly. Setting a truer course on these things seems most fitting in preparing me for the time when the final "bells toll for me,"- in the in-terim the life still in process of being lived more fully.

References
Hemmingway, E (1940). For whom the bell tolls.
In S. Hemmingway (Ed)., <u>Hemmingway on war</u>
(pp. 186-200). New York: Scribner.

CHAPTER 4
A FRENCH CONNECTION

(Originally published in
The Paintsville Herald,
August 27, 2004)

This is my sixth trip to Europe over a span of twenty six years. This trip was unexpected, as I was suddenly activated from the Reserve ranks by the Army for a year stint in Landstuhl, Germany.

Europe has always intrigued me, and in some ways harbored an aura of mystery. Even though my grandparents left Norway for America two generations ago, my personal connection to Europeans has always seemed very questionable. Perhaps the combination of language barriers, cultural differences and perceived antagonisms between Europeans and Americans has left me feeling like an "outsider".

A recent experience at St. Vith, Belgium seems to have altered my thinking considerably about fitting into the European landscape. I visited the old hospital which had served as the headquarters for General Clarke at the beginning of the Battle of the Bulge. Here I followed the path of the 106th Infantry Division which ended up being encircled by the German Army in a fight for its life. In seeing the memorial to the 106th in St Vith, I learned about the tragic demise of a 15,000 strong Division. In the border town of Schoenberg, I spoke to an elderly woman who ran a restaurant. Using her daughter as an interpreter, she recalled how the captured American soldiers of the 106th were marched into her town – the largest surrender of American soldiers since the Civil War, some 10,000 strong.

Retracing the steps of the 106th, seeing the monuments erected on Belgium soil in memory of Americans defending St. Vith and the surrounding area touched me. I saw a chapter of painful European history where Americans had struggled and expended their blood alongside Europeans. For the first time in my travels through Europe, I had found a niche where I, as but one representative from my cultural heritage, could identify with the peoples of Europe in a personal and meaningful way.

After that trip, my fiancé and I went sightseeing in Paris. A French couple offered their assistance, given our struggle to read the menu at an outdoor restaurant. All through our meal we talked casually with them about many topics to include French attitudes toward Americans. The French gentleman wanted to make it clear that despite disagreements about recent American policies, the French people felt a special bond with Americans. He noted the French remember very clearly what American soldiers did for them by storming the beaches of Normandy, and ultimately liberating Paris and the rest of France.

Here all this time I had assumed the French generally disliked Americans, based on what I had heard from Americans who had traveled to France and the media in recent years. But, this man helped to dispel my preconceived assumptions, placing current differences into the larger historical context. Sitting there in that Parisian restaurant, I felt a surprising connection with the French people, as well as affiliation with another piece of European culture and history. It hit home to me that fellow Americans and soldiers from my parent's generation had not been forgotten and, in fact, still honored for the enormous sacrifice made on behalf of France. It's amazing what can happen so innocently on a balmy evening in Paris by a French couple unwittingly acting as good will emissaries.

It is unfortunate that the joining of forces in monumental battles consuming thousands of lives serves as a point of connection. For myself, I can only hope this discovery will lead to other tangible treasures which deepen these newly established bonds of affiliation and kinship.

CHAPTER 5
THE ANGEL BESIDE ME

Being with her like that mattered more than anything else I could think of. And in choosing to be with her I saw a possibility that had never been so clear before: I could leave behind the "mourning veteran" and his preoccupation with the meaninglessness of things, all of which had kept me aloof. Instead I could be there, available for another human being (Egendorf, 1985, p. 168).

The military deployment was a particularly rough year for me from a psychological standpoint. It involved an uprooting of what I had grown comfortable and accustomed with. This came about through an involuntary call-up for a year of active duty with the Army, being assigned to a military hospital in Landstuhl, Germany.

Needless to say, I was very ill-prepared for such a radical change of pace. My private practice as a clinical psychologist had been doing very well, considering the fact I had gone out on my own just a year prior. The balance between spending time with my fiancé and my children from a previous marriage had harmonized to a level I was satisfied with. Even hassles with my ex-spouse had assumed a place of limited importance in that it had become much easier to avoid direct confrontations.

But one call from the Army was all it took to shake up my world dramatically. At fifty years of age, it seemed rather unnatural to be pulled away from loved ones, my job, and the rural surroundings of Eastern Kentucky. Even so, at the time it occurred in March 2004, it was not possible to fully fathom the implications such a transition would entail.

For even a weekend soldier like myself, the call-up produced some initial feelings of excitement and heroic fantasies. Also, the idea of being a dedicated soldier, ready at a moment's notice to defend fellow Americans from the clutches of tyranny and oppression, had a way of minimizing the sacrifices about to be experienced.

Some eight months into the tour of duty, the glamour had fully worn off and been replaced by periods of guilt, boredom, and intense bouts of loneliness. The reality of being apart from those I care about had sunk into the marrow of my emotional joints so acutely that I sometimes questioned whether I could stand much more.

The sanctity of the cause which brought me over there had also soured, having left me to be but another silent protester of an operation that seemed to only mete out suffering and trauma for fellow soldiers, insurgents and Iraqi citizens alike. It brought home to me once again that I did not have the kind of single minded grit, determination and steadfast belief system needed to be a general over the troops and a defender of the mission despite the human cost – the so-called collateral damage.

Having been catapulted into a wartime environment, one large step removed from the actual "front", compelled me to face an aspect of life that essentially did not compute very well at all. It involved the kind of lethal human destruction that could not in my mind be easily justified. Images of mangled, charred bodies of women and children, scattered pieces of flesh of what had been Iraqi police officers, and severed heads of many civilian workers associated with the American cause, had the effect of deflating the grandeur of the American gift of liberty and democratic values.

It is ultimately an age old repetitive story that has swept me up in its wings – the honorable conviction that the enemy represents a noxious vermin and scourge that can best be dealt with by annihilation, by a systematic dismembering of human life itself from those posing a threat and a state of rebellion. One U.S. commander during the war reflected this sentiment by referring to the enemy in Fallujah as "Satan", as he explained why the insurgents had to be decisively defeated.

It is into the midst of such devaluation of life that my very being desperately strove for a counterweight – something that served to infuse my lifeblood with humanistic and life enhancing values. Far from emerging from the lofty peaks of rational arguments and divine inspiration, my salvation had been experienced from a very human, yet very angelic voice - a tender touch, and a pervasive kindness that took hold of me more powerfully than any vise grip could ever do.

Judy represented for me an isle of peace and tranquility that was as removed from the horrific events in Iraq as one could possibly imagine. In fact, she lacked a fundamental understanding of how people could kill one another and feel good about it, no matter what the context. She had a hard enough time dealing with a "hunter's need" to gun down a "defenseless" animal, such as a deer. She essentially placed a very high premium on life itself in all its forms, inclined to support its preservation whenever possible. Her stance appeared to my mind to be the heartbeat of reason saturated with compassion. She really seemed like a female version of Henry David Thoreau making her way through the meadow with the least offensive of steps.

Judy and I have been an item now for well over seven years – having married recently. She has faithfully stood by me during a time when my divorce remained highly conflicted, and when contact with my children was frequently peppered with complications and challenges. She worked hard to avoid imposing herself on my kids. She also remained willing to accept the limitations of our time together, due to bi-weekly visitations with my kids. Through it all she never wavered in her devotion and care, having an uncanny ability to build me up as a man in a variety of ways. It just seemed to be imbedded in her nature to be steadfast regarding the permanency and positive aspects of our relationship.

Still, Judy and I had never been tested before with a lengthy separation as occurred over the year of deployment. We had barely been apart for more that a couple of days at any given time. We had shared so many moments and occasions with each other that neither one of us could really imagine what it would be like to be apart for an entire year. It was only after I had relocated to Germany for a few weeks that the reality of the separation really started to take hold. This even reached a surreal level where the time away assumed a quality of disproportion, like it would never end.

I was struck by how quickly we both started to remember things about our relationship that seemed to serve as tendons holding our past experiences with each other to our present apartness. I wrote the following in one e-mail. *"You went absolutely stark raving wild with e-mails. They were all very engaging, funny, and endearing. You have such a way of pumping up my spirits...I really enjoyed our phone call this evening and 12:00 noon your time. I was glad to impart some positive news about my living quarters. Sometimes when we talk, it almost seems like you are next door, and I can just turn the corner and there you'll be, just as fresh and perky as ever. Yes, I too have enjoyed the things we do together, as with watching movies all cozy on the couch or floor..."*

Judy responded by noting, *"I'm glad you enjoyed my e-mails. It is 8 p.m. here, 2 a.m. there, so hopefully you are already in bed...We plan to go to the "Sipp" tomorrow night to see the Butterfly Effect. I'll let you know if it is good. I know I will wish you were there too – eating popcorn with me and sharing a cherry diet coke, and then me sneaking my shoeless foot into your lap and acting surprised when you start massaging it."*

I am so exceedingly grateful to have had this link with a special person removed from the war. The daily correspondence we shuttled back and forth provided a refuge for me, keeping me connected to the uplifting qualities of life in such stark contrast to the horrifying realities of death and destruction in the combat zone, and the haunting memories resurfacing away from the front. It is hard to know how I would have fared without her affectionate hold on what is best in me.

References
Egendorf, A. (1985). <u>Healing from the war: Trauma &</u>
<u>transformation after Vietnam.</u> Boston, MA:
Shambhala Publications, Inc.

CHAPTER 6
TRIALS OF PUBLISHING ON ABU GHRAIB WHILE ON ACTIVE DUTY

The military is perhaps not the best career choice for someone bent on the vigorous exercise of civil liberties. As countless drill sergeants have informed their new recruits, "We're here to defend democracy- -not to practice it." Qualities valued by an open society- -respect for the individual, independent thinking, skepticism about leaders, the nobility of principled dissent- -do not tend to thrive in a military environment. For obvious reasons, self-sacrifice, discipline, order and obedience to authority tend to be emphasized instead. For every Tom Cruise who wishes it were otherwise, there's a Jack Nicholson to bark at him, "You can't handle the truth!"(Falvo, 2003, pp. 1-2).

Try as I might, I cannot seem to shake loose from an unsettling period which commenced last summer. This occurred during a year long deployment with the U.S. Army as a clinical psychologist.

The trouble all began in the aftermath of the Abu Ghraib scandal, a time when a number of us Army mental health types were privately expressing disbelief and anger that such a thing could happen. My boss and I in fact had several conversations about Abu Ghraib - ones where we seemed to share similar sentiments of shame that our American military system had been involved at levels that could only be guessed at.

I explained to my fiancé in June 2004 some of this dialogue and interaction with my boss. *"I had an interesting talk with my boss. This war is really taking its toll on her. She is really in need of leaving and doing something different – seen too many maimed soldiers. She had heard about the Zimbardo study at Stanford, and in fact the study has been talked about a lot amongst some of her military psychology colleagues as of late. She is going to bring me some materials on it."* The study she had referred to was one where the behavior of assigned guards and inmates was observed in a controlled setting – this correlating to what occurred at Abu Ghraib.

This eventually led to an inspired moment of casting "caution to the wind" by my fervent request to be reassigned to Abu Ghraib. After all, I had prior prison work experience as a psychologist and deeply embedded beliefs about the humane treatment of prisoners. Little did I know that before the year was out, I would probably become one of the Army psychologists least likely to be selected for such an assignment.

I figured one way of coming to grips with Abu Ghraib was to write about it. What started out as a fairly modest endeavor ultimately evolved into a research project which took up a number of my weekends. At first, it was my intention to write down some of my own thoughts about Abu Ghraib, keeping it at more of a personalized reaction. But, psychologist that I am, my interest was piqued to explore how such abusive treatment could be understood psychologically. This led to my incorporation into the paper a few theories and experimental studies in psychology which provided some scientific hardiness to the experiential components.

My excitement about the paper led me to send an e-mail to a psychologist connected with the Middle East/North African Psychology conference in Dubai, United Arab Emirates. My e-mail from June 15, 2004 read, *"I have followed some the situation of prisoner abuse in Iraq and am just completing an article on this, focusing on some psychological theories that may shed some light on how these kinds of things happen. This one is a bit more research based than the first article. Certainly Zimbardo's study has been useful to include in putting this paper together."*

By the time all was said and done, a twenty page paper had emerged with about twenty nine references in the Bibliography. Thinking that the most arduous part of the task had been completed, I now prepared to run the paper through Army channels as a prelude to seeking publication.

Since I knew one of the editors and officers of the Military Psychology division of the American Psychological Association, I decided to get an idea from him about whether this kind of article would fit with their journal. I wrote, *"I am just now completing a 20 page paper on Abu Ghraib. Am drawing from four psychological theories including Zimbardo and Milgram. There are about 26 references at the end. This seems to have some bearing on military psych journals. What do you think, is it worth running by the Military Psych Journal? Do you have time to proof it."*

He responded two days later on Aug 9, 04, stating, *"I will be delighted to review your paper. Just send it along as an email attachment when you are ready and I'll get to work. I am also attaching a copy of the latest div. 19 newsletter that contains an article on the topic by Paul Bartone. You might find it useful."*

I enthusiastically extended my gratitude by noting, *"Thanks for getting back so quick, and for your willingness to review my paper…our Psychology consultant recently has relocated. Am trying to get up with the incoming consultant for the internal review. I will keep you posted when the paper has been approved and ready to send your way."*

It was a rather rude awakening to discover that there are limits to academic freedoms in the Army. One simply does not write an innocent enough looking paper pertaining to some aspect of the military, and then shoot it off to a potential publisher. The consequences could be considerable as the weight of the Uniform Code of Military Justice might be invoked. This code is the same one whose sanctions include incarceration, court-martials, less than honorable discharges and so forth.

The approval process involved a couple of essential steps. First, one had to forward a copy of the manuscript to a consultant in one's specialty domain. The consultant would then review the paper and make recommendations. This could include requirements for changes or even outright rejection. If the paper was approved by the consultant, then one simply had to go to the Public Affairs office for a "rubber stamp" endorsement. The Public Affairs office would read through the document and insure that a disclaimer statement was attached, clarifying that the paper was not a reflection of official Army policy or views. Needless to say, one could sail right through the process unscathed or encounter enormous obstacles.

Having gained easy approval for my first paper (i.e. unrelated to Abu Ghraib), I really expected more of the same with the Abu Ghraib paper. However, a significant change during the interval between the first and second papers was a change in bosses/ Psychology Consultants, one in the same. Compounding the problem was that a gap of time existed between the first boss's departure and the second one's arrival. So, rather than wait until the new boss arrived from his previous duty station in the States, I decided to send the manuscript to him by e-mail. He of course had agreed to review it, even before we had actually met. I now wish I had waited until his arrival, although that may not have altered the outcome significantly anyway.

My new boss wrote me an e-mail from the States, stating a need to forward my manuscript onto a couple of psychologists who specialized in Army prison issues. He explained that his level of experience in the subject matter I wrote on was limited and therefore deserving of greater expertise. Eventually, I got another e-mail from him suggesting we talk further in person about my paper after his arrival. Even then, I sensed an ominous foreboding all was not well with my paper surviving this evaluative process.

Several weeks after my new boss arrived in September, he dropped by to talk about my paper. He had been "under the weather" considerably due to back surgery. We to this point had only become barely acquainted. The situation was far less than optimal, and our initial literary dialogue had many of the "makings" for a disappointing outcome. This turned out to be an understatement.

As my boss stood just inside my doorway, he informed me in short order my paper could not be approved for publication. He indicated that the subject matter of my paper (i.e. focused on Abu Ghraib) was still under investigation and therefore very sensitive. He further noted the Army was not allowing any articles on this topic to be approved for outside publication.

Feeling like I'd been hit with a thunderbolt, I managed to tactfully express my disappointment the Army could not be more open to varying perspectives about major events like Abu Ghraib. I also conveyed that such transparency and willingness for introspection could help an organization like the military make real improvements in the future.

Already devastated, I asked him his opinion about my paper regarding its merits. He told me that it was not really a research paper, noting it was about on the same par as that of a graduate paper being done to satisfy course requirements. He maintained there was nothing original about it, just a restatement of social psychology theories.

My boss also expressed very negative sentiments about the main researcher in my paper (i.e. Zimbardo's *Stanford Prison Experiment*). He emphatically stated that Zimbardo did not put together a good research project, that it was rather "half-baked." He questioned the authenticity and validity of Zimbardo's study. He noted that he had heard Zimbardo speak and considered him to be extremely narcissistic and self-serving. My boss even went so far to note he could not stand this psychologist, and that he was not well liked at all in Army psychology circles – noting Zimbardo had been quite critical of the military.

He went on to question what entitled me to write a paper in an area that I lacked expertise. He noted this kind of paper should be written by those very well attuned to military prisons. My defensive comment of having prior experience working in prison settings did not seem to carry much weight. He told me my other manuscript which focused on my actual work with soldiers and spouses was more fitting for publication, since I had experience with this population.

My boss strongly questioned the sources I was using for establishing what occurred at Abu Ghraib. I noted that I had used a considerable amount of media feedback. He questioned my reliance on that information conduit alone. At this point, I tried to inform him that I also drew from what the military had already acknowledged, and that it was not my intent to question whether more soldiers/officers were involved. I noted I was simply taking the proven, already established information about what had happened at Abu Ghraib.

Following our discussion of the paper, I let my fiancé know what had transpired and how it had impacted me emotionally. *"I sat and remained motionless for about thirty minutes. A lot of things were whirling thru my mind. One thought that came back several times is that this was a contribution I had hoped to make for the good of our country, its reputation, the soldiers dying over there, and humanity at large. In the entire conversation, my new boss did not say one thing about the human factors. Rather, he questioned the validity of what I knew about the abuse at Abu Ghraib, since my sole source was the media. Even when I brought up the fact the military itself has admitted wrongdoing of certain soldiers, he acted like I was on shaky ground with the major premise that prisoner abuse could even be substantiated. For a smallish man, teetering on his spindly legs, he packed quite a punch."*

In another e-mail to my fiancé, I recalled, *"I've had time to process this a bit tonight. It helped for me to pull up the regulations governing release of manuscripts for publication. One provision states that, 'the public released of official DOD (i.e. Dept of Defense) information is limited only as necessary to safeguard information requiring protection in the interest of national security or other legitimate governmental interest...' Little did I know that this article would jeopardize national security or other government interests. This may be the single worst blow I've ever received from the military, impacting a fundamental constitutional right – that being freedom of speech. I don't know that I can just walk away from this one. I will proceed with caution and within appropriate boundaries and established redress procedures. One of my fundamental rights is to write about the problem to my congressman without any reprisals being tolerated, as the regulation reads."*

There are not a lot of things which truly shock me anymore. But, this revelation had the effect of "bowling" me over. I felt as if this did not happen, and that a good night's sleep would chase away the nightmarish moment. It simply did not register that a psychological inquiry into prisoner abuse would be found sufficiently threatening to be squelched. I simply could not fathom a paper purposely depoliticized would stir up such consternation from the military reviewers. It came back to me all the painstaking effort taken to avoid even the slightest insinuation of a cover-up, a "whitewash," and suspicions of higher echelon complicity.

My approach proved so tame that the actual events and personalities that unfolded in the aftermath of Abu Ghraib were not addressed. It had been my endeavor to avoid entanglement anywhere close to the Army's "nerve center" - one where their defensiveness seemed so fortified. I wanted to steer clear of a questioning of the Army's integrity as an institution and instrument of U.S. policy. Instead, the aim was to focus on how any number of well trained soldiers could enact such inhumane treatment of a "captured enemy."

Yet, as a virtual flood of emotions engulfed me, I came to the haunting realization that enough sensitivity over the very topic of Abu Ghraib was out there, even amongst psychologists, that a psychological inquiry by itself created sufficient uneasiness to disallow publication.

I decided to clarify possible misunderstandings with my boss. *"It occurred to me, Sir, following our discussion that I may have given the false impression I was drawing solely from media accounts of the Abu Ghraib situation (i.e. in terms of the factual accounting of what occurred with some detainees). In reality, I drew from some other professional writings which I have attached here for your perusal. These include an article from BMJ (Apr 03), comments for the APA Public Affairs Office (May 04); APA Monitor articles with Psychology Professor Ervin Staub and Dittman (Jul 04); the Military Psychologist Newsletter, Div 19, APA (Summer/Fall 04) with a presidential message and article by LTC Paul Bartone, Ph.D.; and the Psychologist (July 04)."*

The letter continued on: *"Another oversight I made in our*

discussion was not mentioning my intent to seek publication initially with military journals or other periodicals, given the implications of the paper for military personnel. Dr. Brad Johnson, Ph.D., an Associate Editor with the Military Psychology Journal, would have been my first contact person for review of this paper. An alternative plan has been to seek publication, possibly in some psychology related journals or periodicals, or in non-professional related periodicals. Irrespective of gaining Army approval to pursue publication of this paper, Sir, I consider it important to provide you the above clarifications."

I eventually turned to a trusted confident for some balanced and reliable feedback. I wrote, *"I'm afraid the written work of Abu Ghraib was reviewed and turned down for purposes of seeking publication. Was told the topic is too sensitive at this time. May request a second review of it. Can you tell me what your sense is as to how Zimbardo and his Stanford Study are thought of in military psychology circles? Also do you think that one needs to be an expert on prison psychology matters in order to write about such things? Finally, how useful within psychology literature domain is it to present several psychology theories as a way of explaining a phenomenon like the abuse of prisoners at Abu Ghraib? Would you consider a focus like this to be research or non-research? These are some of the things which came up in the critique."*

After a prolonged period of silence, my esteemed colleague from the Military Psychology Division of the American Psychology Association replied. He noted, *"I have indeed been getting e-mail, so let me apologize. Your last note is printed out and sitting right on my desk top. I have just been swamped after taking 10 days away and going to Switzerland to hike and ride the rails with my father. Had a blast. But, I am inevitably behind now. Thanks for following up, or it may have been even longer before hearing from me!"*

He continued on, *"I was sorry to hear that the Abu Ghraib paper was turned down by the power brokers there. I do appreciate the sensitive nature of the material, but my hunch is your paper was thoughtful and scholarly. I must tell you Mark that this was one of the things I struggled with while active duty. I was relieved to become a civilian again so I could write what I wanted."*

He then turned to the prison study by stating, *"Zimbardo is not held in high regard personally by military psychologists because he has been such a critic of the military, of the current administration, and has not even been overtly supportive of troops serving in conflict areas. However, we all teach his groundbreaking prison study in every intro and social class. You cannot get around the important impact of his work.*

You do not have to be an "expert" in prison psychology to write about the events at the Iraq prison, nor is it at all unusual to interpret or consider recent events in light of established psychological theory and research. In fact, it is one of the most common forms of scholarly writing, apart from empirical research. So, to those parts of the critique of your work, I would have to say, sounds like bull_____. And, probably delivered by someone incompetent in your field. This always infuriated me."

He continued on to suggest, *"Options? This is a tough situation Mark because a lot of it hinges on your long term plans. If you want to stay active duty and do the full time career in the military, then you would need to be more cautious. They could make your life hard if you are seen as noncompliant with regulations. It also depends on where you plan to submit your work. If in military journal, you would need to be more cautious about seeking approval. Psych journal? Probably less likely to ever be read by anyone you currently work for."*

"Just some thoughts Mark. I am delighted to know you are still working and enjoying the scholarly side of your psych career."

Even prior to this setback, I had been having trouble enough dealing with the level of destruction and loss of human life from the war, as well as shame associated with events like Abu Ghraib which served to discredit the presence American soldiers held in Iraq.

Now, with this latest issue, my position in the military became more tarnished and questionable. I felt compelled to ask myself whether I could continue to function on active duty while my voice as an American had been suppressed. Too many historical images flooded my mind of repressive regimes where "speaking out" bore dire consequences.

My agonizing and disappointment inevitably led me to the broader and more troubling issue of *freedom of speech* in the military. It is odd that in my twenty nine years with the military this issue of "free speech" never had emerged like it did in this case. There have been times, as far back as my active duty in the mid-70's, that my own individual preferences and sense of self was violated by higher ranking soldiers. In my youthful years with the Army, when forced to "knock out" pushups or "beat my boots," I had times of barking out the count - full of anger and indignation to the tyrannical sergeant standing over me.

There was even a time while on Reserve duty in Panama that I came very close to insubordination. I reacted strongly to a high ranking enlisted soldier who bluntly ordered me to take off a backpack that did not conform to the military dress. I am still grateful to another soldier standing by who placed his hand on my shoulder, encouraging me to let it go, that it was not worth my career to rear up at this "crusty," old sergeant bent on total conformity.

As provocative as these encounters were, I ultimately accepted the fact this was part of wearing the uniform. There would simply be times when superiors would exercise their authority in an overbearing manner, and soldiers like me would again have to let go of our individualistic leanings.

These personal struggles with the authority structure in the military seemed in a different class altogether from this current problem related to military regulations. The Abu Ghraib paper was not a challenge to military authority like the above examples. It was rather a coherent and scholarly piece of writing intended to psychologically examine a series of events in a military run prison.

The question which loomed large was how many other enlisted soldiers and officers had been prevented from publishing their research and individual views of military matters, despite their commitment to solid scholarship and actual events they were familiar with. How much inside information from those much more knowledgeable than myself, such as with high ranking officers in the field or command centers, remained sequestered – far from the reach of public awareness? Just how much had the direction or this current war, as well as previous ones, been guided in a particular manner as a result of this muzzling effect? Indeed, the operative principle was that those most directly involved with the war, many laying their very lives on the alter, were the very ones required to keep their views and knowledge of the war private and out of the public eye.

This should not be confused with the protection of classified material that could jeopardize the overall mission or safety of soldiers in the field. Rather, this has to do with officers and enlisted soldiers being prevented from expressing their views and insider knowledge of military affairs that, if aired, might serve to redirect how and when and where military operations would occur.

I ultimately decided that it would be too unconscionable to go along with the order not to publish. Still, it seemed prudent to work as best as possible within the system, requesting a second opinion of my Abu Ghraib proposal. So, knowing that I was now sticking my neck out, I met with the head of the whole psychiatric department. He was not any different from previous consultations in that he seemed to extend an open, thoughtful exchange. He carefully read the letter I had written to my boss in requesting a second opinion. He even expressed understanding of my passionate claim that it seemed to be my very duty and service to my country to carry forward with this appeal.

In the past this officer had an unusual receptivity to philosophical and moralistic discussions about various applications of psychiatry (and psychology) in the military. In fact, he could often take the lead in stepping out into the "ozone" so to speak, becoming rather free-wheeling and "maverick-like" with his ideas. He could also be amazingly candid about some of the inner workings and political "goings-on" within the Army hospital, along with the frustrations he experienced routinely in attempting to run the department.

This irreverent and brutally honest part of his makeup took on a "backseat" posture when real decisions had to be made that involved others in the "chain of command." In this respect, he was strongly inclined toward a conservative and rather cautious style of leadership. This proved to be true in the way he dealt with the letter I intended to send to my boss.

He forthrightly suggested to me that I not submit such an appeal to my boss. Without taking into account the personality of my boss, his express concern was this could be viewed as a challenge to my boss's authority. He conveyed his belief that the letter could lead to a conflicted situation that could only cause grief for me in particular. While allowing me the choice of how to proceed, he noted that the safer approach was to publish once I completed my year of active duty. I took it to mean that my career as a reserve officer would be better safeguarded by maintaining a low posture.

Even as this meeting came to a conclusion, I was convinced there was no turning back – that I would "cast caution to the wind" and carry on with my "sacred mission." My final words to him likely left him with the impression that I was bound to proceed with this appeal regardless of the personal costs. He seemed to show respect and understanding of my "higher calling" while finishing off with words of concern for my future in the military. I ended up leaving the meeting with more internal uncertainty than I expected, or wanted to occur.

Shortly after this exchange I sent off an e-mail to a previous boss. I explained how the Abu Ghraib paper had been turned down. A portion of it read, *"Based on the above, I prepared a letter to _____________ requesting a second review of the paper at the MEDCOM (i.e. medical command). I did this after consulting with _____________ at the Public Affairs Office. She advised me of this process of asking for a second review. I consulted with _____________ (i.e. the head of the behavioral health department) as a final step prior to submitting the letter. He was not favorable of the idea, feeling it might promote some unnecessary tensions. He thought it might be better to wait until I was done with my year deployment. But, he respected my concerns about wanting to publish while still on active duty, and some of the principles at stake (i.e. academic freedoms, etc.). So, he suggested I consult with you which I agree is a good idea. Part of the reason I say this is because you and I had talked several times about the paper and the issues involved."*

It was during this period of internal debate about the course to take (i.e. October 7, 2004), I drafted a letter intended for congressional review. It went as follows: *"I am an Army Reserve Officer who has been activated for one year to Landstuhl, Germany, ending in March 2005. As a clinical psychologist, I have been assigned to work in the outpatient psychiatry unit, Landstuhl Regional Medical Center. Three days a week I have been "farmed out" to the Baumholder Health Clinic, home of the 2nd Brigade, 1st Armored Division. Working these two sites has brought me in contact with a number of soldiers and their spouses, many soldiers having returned to Baumholder in July 2004 from Iraq.*

During this past year, I have been doing some writing on my own time. My intent has been to submit these ten to twenty page papers for publication. One article dealing with psychologists' potential role in the provision of diplomatic negotiations in the Middle East is currently being reviewed by the staff of an online publication. Of course, any article written has to be approved by a Psychology Consultant in the Army prior to submission to any publishing company.

The reason for this letter is that a paper I wrote pertaining to the Abu Ghraib scandal was not allowed to move for possible publication. The Psychology Consultant…informed me that any paper written about the Abu Ghraib situation was not being approved for pursuit of publication. He noted this was due to the sensitive nature of the topic, along with the ongoing investigation. He also maintained that he had my paper reviewed by a few knowledgeable specialists familiar with the 'military prison' domain.

The twenty page paper I wrote highlights four different psychological theories that provide a possible explanation for prisoner abuse at Abu Ghraib prison. Interwoven into this theoretical paper is an analysis of how 'dehumanization' of other persons can occur, making some comparisons between the Nazis' treatment of the Jews and some American soldiers' treatment of prisoners at Abu Ghraib. Based on certain theories in Social Psychology, a major contention of this paper is that non-pathological, decent individuals can end up committing dehumanizing acts toward others when placed in certain adverse circumstances. One of the key studies used in the paper was "Zimbardo's Stanford Prison Experiment" with students acting as prisoners or guards in a mock prison over a two week period.

Having been affiliated with the Army for 27 years, it is not customary for me to take military grievances to a congressional level – this time serving as a first. However, the issues at stake here seem in my mind to warrant such an approach. My concern is that academic liberties are being unduly restricted when it pertains to topics the Army may perceive as damaging to their image. It is my conviction sensitive topics like Abu Ghraib should be openly assessed and scrutinized by individuals both within and without the military system. A suppression of such papers as mine seems to perpetuate a 'fortress' mentality where greater understanding of inhumane treatment of prisoners cannot be achieved, making it more difficult to really develop solid strategies to prevent the reoccurrence of these events later on.

In my judgment, a failure to thoroughly evaluate such deviant behavior of American soldiers at Abu Ghraib prison serves to potentially endanger the lives of American soldiers, as well as those affiliated with the U.S. there. It also serves to perpetuate attitudes in the military which foster future prisoner abuse. The very task set out for the American military of legitimizing themselves and their cause in Iraq thus has been markedly compromised and undermined. Finally a failure to explore different research findings and psychological theories on Abu

Ghraib makes it difficult for an understanding of possible weaknesses and temptations toward abuse of others that may be a part of the human makeup – the possibility then looming for increased risks of abuse within the ranks of a soldier population.

It is therefore my request the Army decision to disallow the seeking of publication of the above mentioned paper on Abu Ghraib prison be investigated, and if so deemed, overturned. Your assessment of this matter is most appreciated."

The clarion warning from the head of the behavioral health department ultimately held sway. Very reluctantly I did not request a review of the decision denying publication of the Abu Ghraib paper, nor did the above letter get sent off to my congressman. I chose instead to play it safe, and by the rules, in order to protect myself from an unpleasant and possibly a very self-destructive outcome. It seemed more prudent to refrain from going public for another four months or so until my active duty would be concluded.

References

Falvo, D. G. (2003) The Limits of Free Speech in the Military: Can Public Expressions of Discontent by U.S. Troops in Iraq Be Punished. Retrieved December 10, 2005. http://writ.findlaw.com/commentary.

CHAPTER 7
ABU GHRAIB

A Psychological Search
For How Such Dehumanization
of Detainees Could Occur

NOTE: This paper was denied publication by the U. S. Army until my active duty time was completed in Mar 2005, reportedly due to an ongoing investigation of soldier conduct at Abu Ghraib and the sensitive nature of the subject matter. The only modifications made were the opening quotes by Staub on August 1, 2006. This chapter is retained in its original format while I was still in Germany.

We cannot judge evil by conscious intentions, because psychological distortions tend to hide even from the perpetrators themselves their true intentions. They are unaware, for example, of their unconscious hostility or that they are scapegoating others. Frequently, their intention is to create a "better world," but in the course of doing so they disregard the welfare and destroy the lives of human beings.

Perpetrators of evil often intend to make people suffer but see their actions as necessary or serving a higher good (Staub, 1989 p. 25).

But the people who participated in this mass murder were normal by conventional standards of mental health. In-

terviews and psychological testing found no evidence of mental illness or psychological dysfunction in the Nuremberg defendants and SS criminals (Staub, 1989, p. 91).

Abstract

The abuse of some detainees at Abu Ghraib, Baghdad by some U.S. soldiers has created much distress amongst Americans, leaving in its wake many unanswered questions how this manner of dehumanization of detainees could have occurred. The very values held by many Americans regarding appropriate treatment of prisoners, or detainees, has been markedly put to the test. A psychological inquiry is conducted to assess how such a phenomenon could occur under the United States banner. Two psychological theories and two landmark experimental studies in social psychology are highlighted – all of which have something to say about how humans treat others under certain conditions. These are (a) Zimbardo's Stanford Prison Experiment, (b) In-group & Out-group Dynamics (prompted by Allport's study on Prejudice), (c) Milgram's Obedience to Authority Study, and (d) Girard's Scapegoat Theory. The author challenges common assumptions that dehumanizing actions towards groups of targeted people is best understood when looking at places like Nazi Germany, as opposed to strong democracies like the United States. Additionally, as the above theories and studies suggest, an alternative hypothesis emerges which indicates that more normal, decent individuals can engage in inhumane and cruel behaviors when prompted by certain internal and external conditions.

The events which have unfolded at Abu Ghraib have jolted American sensibilities, and undoubtedly revived memories of other ignoble chapters in our collective history. Once again, as so often occurs in times of war and national crisis, our cherished values of fairness, humaneness, and due process under the law have been raised to a high level of consciousness and debate. The plethora of debasing pictures has had the effect of convincing even many of the skeptics that an as yet undetermined number of American soldiers participated in acts of detainee mistreatment. Many of our minds are now forced to grapple with the reality that certain American soldiers were able to carry out torturous acts against members of a society that we came to liberate from such inhumane treatment. This in turn raises questions once again about the degree to which American values actually get translated into consistent action supportive of these values.

I certainly would not want to suggest that these are easy issues to work through, or that I, as a result of my psychological training, can offer a definitive explanation and resolution of the phenomenon. What can be provided here are a few observations and research findings regarding mistreatment of certain groups of people, attitudes fostering such abuse, and the manner in which a wartime situation may foster a departure from humane treatment of enemy combatants.

My fourteen year old son had an unsettling experience in the classroom this past school year. It occurred during a discussion of how the Americans brought Japan to the negotiating table at the end of World War II. He challenged the view expressed by the teacher that the nuclear bombing of Hiroshima and Nagasaki had to occur in order to save the lives of American soldiers fighting in the Far East. She conveyed to him his questioning of Japanese noncombatants being killed by the thousands was out of bounds, implying that it almost went to the point of violating American values. The most disturbing aspect of this interchange is not that she promoted the view she did – which of course is a common justification of these events – but that my son's dissenting view was dismissed as unpatriotic.

His argument was predicated on one which has direct bearing on the Geneva Convention and the manner in which populations of enemy states should be treated. But, because an exception to the rule had become widely accepted in the American psyche, his argument defending an overarching principle of humaneness did not even get an opportunity to be explored on its merits. A prevailing American sentiment demanded silence from the opposition.

The connecting point between this encounter and the recent events at Abu Ghraib is two fold. For one, it illustrates how the values of a nation are not always consistent with practices and justified sentiments, especially under duress. Highlighted as well is the potential impact individual or group departure from American ideals can have on others exposed to such revisionist thought.

Under my current Army deployment to Germany for the next year, I have had some opportunity to revisit some of the battlefields and monuments to American heroism in World War II. A very highly publicized atrocity occurred during the Battle of the Bulge, one in which it appears a German officer authorized the execution of a number of American prisoners in a small village in Belgium. The officer was tried after the war for this violation of the prevailing laws regarding treatment of prisoners (Whiting, 2000). It was clearly understood on both sides that these soldiers could be legitimately annihilated when they were actively involved in the fight. But, the rules dramatically changed for the protection of the prisoners once they had surrendered or been disarmed. It appears the officer disregarded this standard for possibly reasons of expediency, built up animosity, and/or a desire to break down the will of the enemy.

Naturally, it can be expected that it might be easier for Americans to focus on the mistreatment of our own soldiers than when our soldiers become the perpetrators. It may also be more palatable to justify our own departures from lawful treatment of prisoners of war or detainees than to grant leniency to enemy soldiers or commanders doing the same with our soldiers.

Clearly there are going to be some soldiers who will do the "globalization thing." Because he or she witnessed certain Iraqis engaging in underhanded methods of fighting and killing our soldiers, they more readily conclude that all combative soldiers are in the same mold. This can even project outward to the hatred of all Iraqi society. The enemy now truly becomes the "original folks" we were commissioned to protect.

So, given this line of thinking, enemy detainees can all be considered to be "killers of Americans," the "ilk" of Iraqi society, "Islamic extremist terrorists," and therefore undeserving of normal protections afforded detainees under the Geneva Convention.

It is not necessary to interview one of the charged American soldiers to flush out such sentiments. I can just converse with soldiers back here in Germany to discover similar attitudes, some who have been "down range" and others who have remained in the rear. One fairly common response has been that these detainees do not get in prison for being "nice guys," and being known for playing by the rules. So, this manner of thinking goes on to conclude that these detainees deserve the humiliation and abuse they are getting. Those promoting this line of reasoning seem to be implying that the Geneva Convention should not be considered applicable for a group of combatants with so little respect for human life, and ones known to be so treacherous to our soldiers. Therefore, the soldiers applauding these actions are inclined to side with a group of charged soldiers who are up for court martial, simply regretting these individuals getting caught through such a "stupid" means as taking photographs.

The capacity individuals have to be cruel and tortuous appears to be the result of a psychological process of dehumanizing their victims (Conflict Research Consortium Staff, n.d.; Deutsch, 2000; Maiese, 2003). Our century alone is replete with examples of horrible atrocities committed against others by individuals who bear the appearance of being integrated into mainstream society, have seemingly normal familial relations, and exercising good will toward their fellow citizens. Americans have had the luxury of conducting in depth analysis of German leaders and soldiers in World War II who exhibited this kind of dual personality – intense hostility and hatred being reserved for specific groups, as with Jewish and Armenian people. The highly cultured and nurturing side often seemed intact for other Aryans, especially those within the confines of the "Fatherland."

It is rather anathema to the American persona to think such potential for dehumanizing certain "others" resides not only within our borders, but within the most cultured and seemingly civilized quarters. The treatment rendered to African Americans, Native Americans, and other ethnic groups serves as an unpleasant reminder of the American capacity for devaluing the worth of select groups. Certain well established segments of American society even incorporated biblicized justifications of slavery, and the governmental policies which dehumanized thousands of African Americans (Finkelman, 2003). With this kind of cultural baggage, should we be so caught up with our own state of enlightenment to think that the American capacity to dehumanize others has been permanently amputated?

It is therefore not necessary for Americans to fight in foreign lands in order to exhibit dehumanizing attitudes and treatment of targeted groups. My civilian work as a clinical psychologist in a men's prison has convincingly demonstrated how often prison officials can so readily swing over to a collective view of inmates, thereby devaluing them as human beings. This of course can then translate into practices that unnecessarily fuel conflicts based on correctional officer attitudes of superiority and being obeyed without question, even to the point of inmates being viewed as a markedly lesser class of people.

Staub (2004) notes the more prison rules tend to be dehumanizing, the easier it is for prison officials to consider inmates as being outside the pale of normal humane treatment. I have often wondered about the degree of escalated mistreatment of inmates in the event a psychologist like myself, or visiting teams from corporate office, were not present in the system as a kind of "watchdog" of staff excesses.

A landmark psychological study was conducted in 1971 to assess how "normal," well integrated, college age males would function in a mock two week long prison setting. The participating males, mostly college students, were assigned the task of role playing either a prison guard or an inmate (Zimbardo, 1976).

Several of the nine men assuming the role of guards, despite an apparent lack of prior psychological problems, became increasingly harsh and punitive to the point where role playing prisoners were being mistreated with a variety of tactics thought up by the guards (American Psychological Association – Public Affairs (2004), Dittman, 2004). These included: (a) spraying prisoners with extremely cold carbon dioxide from fire extinguishers, (b) stripping prisoners naked, (c) removing the beds from the cells, (d) lengthy periods of required push-ups, (e) toilet bowl cleaning with bare hands, (f) solitary confinement beyond the allowed one hour time period, (g) periodically leaving the buckets in the cells prisoners used to urinate and defecate in, and (h) arbitrarily giving privileges to some prisoners in order to create prisoner mistrust of each other (Zimbardo, 1999-2004).

Zimbardo (1999-2004) notes that a recent Ph.D. graduate, Maslach, assigned to interview the participants was shocked and repulsed to see prisoners being led on a toilet run with bags over their head and chained together. Even more disturbing to the researchers as a whole were videotapes revealing that "pornographic and degrading prisoner abuse" (1999-2004) was occurring in the middle of the night.

Although the study was designed to last two weeks, it became necessary to discontinue it after only six days. The psychological and physical torment of prisoners had simply become too excessive. This realization for Zimbardo only came about by the challenging feedback of Maslach who found the treatment of prisoners abhorrent (O'Toole, n.d.; Zimbardo, 1999-2004). Four prisoners had become psychologically impaired in the course of those six days and much of the prisoner cohesion had broken down. The guards had gained complete dominance over the depressed and markedly distressed prisoners to the point where utter obedience had been achieved across the board (1999-2004).

Despite Zimbardo's professional experience as a research psychologist, and years after the study having assumed the presidency of the esteemed American Psychological Society (APA), he acknowledged his vulnerability to the role he held as prison superintendent. When intruded upon by an academic colleague while attempting to deal with an anticipated jailbreak, he noted,

> I got really angry at him. Here I had a prison break on my hands. The security of my men and the stability of my prison was at stake, and now, I had to deal with this bleeding-heart, liberal, academic, effete dingdong who was concerned about the independent variable! It wasn't until much later that I realized how far into my prison role I was at that point – that I was thinking like a prison superintendent rather than a research psychologist (Zimbardo, 1999-2004, slide-27).

The central theme of this study - that decent people can become corrupted and inhumane if placed in an environmental setting conducive to abuse of others – has undergone scholastic scrutiny before. William Golding hammered on this in his work, "Lord of the Flies," that has become an oft-read classic amongst many school age adolescents. He forcefully demonstrated the view that school children can become cruel and primitively cannibalistic when placed in an austere environment without any adult guidance.

Preuss, Conrad, & Wildfeuers' (2000) recent movie, The Experiment, is an amplified version and accounting of the Stanford Prison Experiment. As with the actual study, the movie depicts the steady deterioration of moral norms that occurs amongst the prison guards. It provides a visual picture of how the guards increasingly strive to gain complete control over the prisoners, partially as a response to being mocked and not taken seriously by the prisoners. Considerable cinematic license is used, however, where the guards actually imprison or kill the researchers, and ultimately some of them are killed by the prisoners. But, then one does have to wonder what would have happened had the Stanford Prison Experiment not been terminated.

When cultural groups are viewed as profoundly different in mannerisms, customs, and values, greater opportunities are present of interpreting the peculiarities of these differences as signs of inferiority and, if carried far enough, something sub-human. Judgments can readily be mustered where the misunderstood group is assessed as being barbaric, uncivilized, and unpredictably dangerous. Left to its own devices, such "loose cannon" groups can fester and expand like an unwelcome virus.

Did prejudicial attitudes toward their Arab detainees by some of the American soldiers at Abu Ghraib influence their thinking, and ultimately the manner in which the detainees were treated? Schlabach (1998), drawing from the theoretical work on prejudice by the eminent psychologist, Gordon Allport (1954), describes the way in which an in-group and out-group mentality can impact attitudes. She illustrates how even sports fans backing a certain team can identify more with other fans of the same team than with people supporting the opposing team, despite greater similarities with some of the fans of the opposing team. But, she noted, the failure to see these similarities is based on a tendency to lump all of the opposing fan members into one global entity – viewing them all as being just like the rest.

Despite the reality that in-groups are often in a state of hostility toward the out-group, it is not a necessary preconditioned state of affairs. There are times when it has been noted that more positive feelings can be felt toward the out-group, even though preferential treatment for the in-group is likely to exist (Allport, 1954; Brewer, 1999; Pettigrew, 1999). This would help to explain how people from varied groups can in many cases co-exist next to each other and potentially have a high level of cooperation. Other factors may need to be assessed to better understand the process by which hostile attitudes emerge toward the out-group.

Still, it is rather common to commit what is known as a "group attribution error" where the entire opposing group is perceived as just like those worst offenders in their group (Forsyth, 1997). As in the case with Abu Ghraib, a natural tendency would be to view all the detainees as being equally treacherous and guilty of atrocities (Staub, 2004) against American soldiers.

As I discovered going through Army Basic Training in 1973, a concerted in-group cohesion is strongly fostered while instilling almost simultaneously a strong repugnance of the enemy out there. Back then, most of these negative references were directed toward the North Vietnamese. The aim in fact was to find this out-group as being antithetical to our way of life, and therefore deserving of death through our actions on the battlefield. This devaluing process toward the enemy becomes highly problematic when members of the enemy group assume a detainee status. Just, as with the German officer referred to earlier, American soldiers run the risk of depersonalizing and dehumanizing the enemy (Staub, 2004) unless they undergo a cognitive shift. This would likely involve a move to consider detainees more individually and uniquely, one from the other.

The ongoing investigation at Abu Ghraib revolves around a theme of involvement, be it a small band of aberrant soldiers or one involving higher echelons of authority. Perhaps the most famous study on conformity may have something to contribute to this analysis of detainee abuse, particularly if those carrying out the degrading actions believed they were following directives, whether explicitly or implicitly.

Motivated in part by the Holocaust and the Nuremburg trials, especially Eichmann's defense of just following orders,

Milgram (1961) conducted some studies on the manner in which individuals obey authority figures. The most celebrated research involved two individuals showing up at a testing center at the same time. One of the subjects would be strapped into a chair with an electrode attached to an arm. The remaining subject was assigned the role of the teacher in an adjoining room. The teacher's role was to read a list of two word pairs. The "learner" strapped in the chair was expected to repeat back those word pairs correctly. If the response was incorrect, the teacher was instructed to administer 15 volts of electricity to the learner by flipping a switch. The amount of voltage would increase by 15 volt increments for each additional incorrect response. The teacher was never forced to continue with the increased amounts of shock. They were simply told the experiment called for them to proceed regardless of concerns about excessive electrical shocks being administered to the learners. What the teachers did not know is that the learners were actually working with the experimenter and were not really getting shocked (Goret, Zega, Voss & Fawcett-Hammalian, 1998; The Milgram Experiment, n.d).

This routine was repeated with many different pairs of individuals made up of seemingly normal people coming from blue collar, managerial and professional backgrounds. The surprising results showed that all the teachers compliantly raised the levels of voltage up to 300 volts, and that 65% went the extra distance to the maximum 450 volts. It demonstrated that the majority of participants would obediently inflict maximum harm to the learners, even when concerned about the welfare of the learners (Goret, Zega, Voss & Fawcett-Hammalian, 1998; The Milgram Experiment, n.d.).

The implications have been enormous in terms of what this might mean regarding blind obedience to authority figures to the point of carrying out acts of violence and cruelty. It also implies that it may not always be fringe, antisocial elements of society who carry out atrocities against others, but rather in addition well integrated, mainstream persons.

The applicability of these findings to the situation at Abu Ghraib still remains difficult to gauge. However, it may go a long way in providing a partial explanation of some of the abusive treatment of detainees, particularly if the soldiers involved in the abuse ultimately reveal a belief they were following orders, directives, or expectations of higher level authorities. In addition, it remains to be seen whether some of these abusive soldiers harbored mixed feelings about their acts, but that compliance won out.

Years ago when studying political science, I recall the profound impact of some of the Nazi propaganda films, depicting Jewish persons as being exceedingly crude and animalistic in their practices of killing cattle. The films graphically displayed the way in which the animals would have their throats slit wide open, thereby forcing the blood to gush spasmodically (i.e. known as "Shechitah"). The head of the animal would cast about wildly suggestive of horrendous pain during the dying process (Hornshoj-Moller, 1997; Unser Wille, 1940). So, by appearance, this could easily be construed as a blatantly grotesque form of animal cruelty. Of course, it was not well explicated to the viewers that this was the optimal way to satisfy religious requirements – a viable means of eliminating blood from the meat.

Films such as these went a long way in painting a distorted picture of Jews as inhuman and frightening when allowed to infiltrate normal civilized society. This method of loosening the soil helped greatly in leading a nation-state to gather up this "menacing force" and ultimately implement the "final solution." The Nazi propaganda film, "Der ewige Jude" purposely highlighted this ritual slaughtering of animals in order to shock the German audience into seeing the Jewish people as unworthy of humane treatment (Hornshoj-Moller, 1997; Unser Wille, 1940). The deprivation of human dignity of these skeleton-like starving Jews – most blatant by the time they entered the gas chambers, or were shot into mass graves – further accentuated the perception their executioners had of them being something other than human and deserving of inhumane treatment (Pogonowski, n.d.).

There are multiple ways of trying to psychologically comprehend how the Jewish people became the recipients of so much hatred and violence. Girard's (1977) development of a "scapegoat theory" is one approach in making sense of a particular group being so targeted. He argued that humans have a "memetic" (i.e. imitative) impulse to desire what another group wants. As a way of ameliorating the conflict between such groups, a united front can be established by targeting a scapegoat to receive the bulk of the blame. A splintered society can thus coalesce together by directing negative energy and hatred outward onto another group. The scapegoating mechanism is activated most readily under the following conditions: (a) collapse of order and differentiation like political conflict, (b) searching of parties responsible for assaulting the order, (c) chosen victims already viewed with suspicion like a class of outsiders, and (d) uniting against the scapegoat which helps to create inward solidarity (Girard, 1977; Michael, n.d.).

In keeping with the above conditions, the Nazi machinery took great pains to explain to the public how the Jews had managed to undermine their culture, economy, morals, and the very fabric of German society (Eitzen, 1936). This came in the wake of a fragmented society following the First World War. The Jewish people were easily identified as a marginalized group already given the seething anti-Semitism so prevalent in the country. By blaming a group considered to be quasi-outsiders for all that was awry in Germany, it served to avoid the more painful route of finding fault with fellow countrymen.

The mistreatment rendered to some of the detainees at Abu Ghraib differs dramatically from what occurred in the Nazi concentration camps, as large numbers were not exterminated. However, in terms of the humiliation, psychologically induced distress, debasing and inhumane treatment – however limited the number of detainees and abusive soldiers involved – the correlation with the Nazi camps has a more familiar ring.

A scapegoating dynamic may have been operative in this prison, despite very different scenarios between Nazi Germany sixty some years ago and an American run prison camp in Iraq. It appears the four conditions for scapegoating Gerard listed may have been present. It can certainly be noted that Americans in Iraq had encountered some degree of a breakdown of order in Iraq as indicated by the number of friendly casualties. It would not have been too hard searching for a party responsible for this lack of order. Clearly, incarcerated detainees would be very suspect for wrongdoing and also thought to be very foreign. Finally, the detainees served as a reachable target in meting out hostilities which could also potentially bring about greater bonding among soldiers.

The determination to maximize the debasement is all the more revealing by going for the jugular – compelling the detainees to engage in activities most in violation of their values and religious beliefs in order to survive. Who other than such a hated group of Arabs – ones directly associated with terrorists and other opposition forces responsible for American deaths – would become the brunt of such dehumanizing treatment. Indeed, the impulse to dehumanize these detainees was so powerful that it overrode any natural fear soldiers would have of being discovered and severely punished for obvious disregard of the Geneva Convention and the Uniform Code of Military Justice.

In summary, two theories and two pivotal experimental studies have been introduced that may correspond to some degree with the abuses of detainees at Abu Ghraib. These include, (a) Zimbardo's Stanford Prison Experiment, (b) In-group, Out-group dynamics inspired by Allport's work on Prejudice, (c) Milgram's Obedience to Authority study, and (d) Girard's Scapegoat Theory. At best, these theories may provide some illumination onto the Abu Ghraib landscape regarding psychological factors leading to the acts of mistreatment of detainees. As is so often the case with theoretical frameworks, there are limitations to their explanatory prowess of certain life events. In the case of Abu Ghraib, it is conceivable that pieces of all these theories may have been operative and/or non-operative, as well as some other unmentioned and perhaps unearthed factors.

Some recent psychological literature renders support to Zimbardo and Milgrams's central thesis that decent, humane individuals with an absence of prior psychopathology can commit acts of inhumanity and blatant cruelty when certain internal and systemic conditions are present (American Psychological Association – Public Affairs, 2004; Dittmann, 2004a, 2004b; Staub, 2004). When soldiers involved with Abu Ghraib are themselves subjected to high levels of stress – being very aware how their fellow soldiers are potential casualties at any time - the dehumanization of a confined enemy who can easily be viewed as causing a threat to the lives of Coalition forces becomes a more likely prospect. This line of reasoning thus suggests that more normal individuals are capable of acts of atrocity and dehumanization, as opposed to such acts solely being the playground of the social deviants and psychopaths. It is a shuddering thought that the divide between the Nazis, Khmer Rouge, and other organized groups responsible for dehumanization and genocide, juxtaposed to democratically oriented Americans may not be as great as we would like to believe. It is also most unsettling to contemplate the possibility that human beings in general, regardless of nationality and political order, can sink into depraved, inhumane, and ultimately genocidal behavior – perhaps at times without even realizing what has happened.

It is worth noting that personality factors can impact how individuals choose to respond to situations conducive to dehumanizing acts. Bartone (2004) noted that some individuals in positions of authority do not submit to the pressures of inhumane actions, even when it may be occurring around them. They manage to exercise strength of character and convictions, avoiding the acts of brutality by many of their peers. The interactive effects between personality factors, and environmental ones (i.e. as depicted by Zimbardo, Milgram, Girard and Schlabach), certainly deserve further research and analysis in the future.

The prospect that a Zimbardo(ian), Milgram(ian) and Gerard(ian) world view – what with its rather bleak understanding of human nature – may harbor some accurate insights about the human propensity for dehumanization and cruelty toward designated persons is not very palatable. It suggests that systemic variables and influences of group dynamics play a critical role outdistancing individual corruptions and evil inclinations. It also suggests that even better systems of government and institutions can potentially be undermined by the lack of accountability and oversight. Even more frightening, it may also suggest the enemy to democracy, individual freedom, and dignity/rights of individuals lurks more within the courtyard than without. The specter of Conrad's (1963, p. 117) assertion about the protagonist's fall into depravity (i.e.

in Heart of Darkness) once again looms on the horizon with the hideous words, "the horror, the horror" - suggestive of a malevolent force within all of us that can get activated.

Following the conclusion of the Second World War, there was a piece of history which received little attention from the history books in Germany. German children simply learned little about what happened in their country when the Third Reich came to power. It was considered too shameful and emotionally distressing to even look squarely at the factual account of Hitler's regime (Brandenburg, 1990). It seemed easier to act as if this period of German history, horrifying as it was, barely existed. Consequently, it was not possible for the post-war generation to learn very much from the mistakes made and how to avoid them in the future.

It remains a point of discussion the degree to which Americans have processed periods of their own history when "normal people" engaged in dehumanizing and extremely cruel actions toward fellow human beings of particular ethnic backgrounds, political persuasions, religious orientations, and national origins – all the while often convinced they were acting in good faith and with a clean conscience Even though I am unaware of major historical events being kept out of American history books, it remains questionable about the accuracy of some historical accounts, especially when possible acts of inhumanity may have been committed by certain American groups , governmental entities and/or societal forces. Perhaps the approach some Germans have taken facing their own "demons" is not so far removed from our own.

The appearance of Abu Ghraib on the American radar screen is another opportunity to learn something about ourselves, and how dehumanization can emerge and acquire some institutional life in a democratic society with such lofty values. Far from being an isolated event, it challenges Americans to look deeply into an American past checkered with not only acts of dehumanization and atrocity, but also justifications for these events within our own psyche. It also challenges Americans to reassess what such principles of fair play are all about, as with the Geneva Convention, when we are facing off with very violent and seemingly barbaric opponents.

The final words are far from spoken regarding Abu Ghraib and how such a thing came about. The theories and studies presented in this paper provide some plausible psychological explanations regarding the events which occurred there. The fact that there has been some empirical research behind these theories and studies provides for theoretical hardiness. Still, further research is needed in order to build upon or challenge their assertions.

In the meantime, the military would be well served to incorporate the above theoretical approaches into their training of soldiers, NCO's and officers. Recognition that dehumanizing behavior is not so foreign to the psyche of American soldiers as perhaps previously thought is an important step forward – owning the reality of being vulnerable. Such sensitization of the issues could in turn act as a springboard for vigorous discussion about the events at Abu Ghraib and safeguards to prevent such a reoccurrence. Hopefully this would also open up healthy dialogue about the application of the Geneva Convention in a number of diverse situations, including ones where deviations from the tenets of the Convention seem justifiable.

References
Allport, G. W. (1954). <u>The nature of prejudice.</u>
Reading, MA: Addison-Wesley.

American Psychological Association – Public Affairs (2004, May). How psychology can help explain the Iraqi prisoner abuse. Retrieved August 07, 2004 from http://www.apa.org/pubinfo/prisonerabuse.html

Bartone, P.T. (2004). The need for positive meaning in military operations: Reflections on Abu Ghraib. The Military Psychologist, 20(2), 17-21.

Brewer, M. B. (1999). The psychology of Prejudice: Ingroup love or outgroup hate? Journal of Social Issues.

Brandenburg, M. (1990). Quest: Searching for Germany's Nazi past. Novato, CA.: Presidio Press.

Conflict Research Consortium Staff (n.d.). Dehumanization. University of Colorado: Conflict Research Consortium.

Conrad, J. (1973), Heart of Darkness. London: Penguin Books. (Original work published 1902).

Deutsch, M. (2000). "Justice and conflict." In The handbook of conflict resolution: theory and practice. San Francisco: Jossey-Bass.

Dittmann, M. (2004). Psychological science offers clues to Iraqi prisoner abuse. Monitor on Psychology, 35(7), 13.

Dittmann, M. (2004). What makes good people do bad things? Monitor on Psychology, 35(6), 68-69.

Eitzen, K. H. (1936). Zehn Knuppel wider die Judenknechte. Unser Wille und Weg, 6, 309-310.

Finkelman, P. F. (2003). <u>Defending slavery - Proslavery</u> <u>thought in the old South: A brief history with documents.</u> Bedford: St Martins.

Forsyth, D.R. (1997). <u>Group dynamics: Relations between</u> <u>groups</u>. Class notes presented to students at college (unknown location).

Girard, R. (1977). <u>Violence and the sacred</u>. Baltimore, MD: Johns Hopkins Press.

Goret, M., Zega, A., Voss, L. & Fawcett-Hammalian, G. (Compiled by). (1998). Stanley Milgram. In Eon Solutions Ltd. <u>Retrieved June 12, 2004, from</u> <u>http://members.tripod.com/mikeg531/MikeG531.htm</u>

Hornshof-Moller, S. (1997, March). <u>Using authentic Nazi</u> <u>propaganda in teaching the Holocaust: Problems, possibilities,</u> <u>dangers and experiences.</u> Paper presented at the 27th Annual Scholar's Conference on the Holocaust and the Churches, Tampa, FL.

Golding, W. (1959). <u>Lord of the flies</u>. New York: Perigree

Maiese, M. (2003). <u>Dehumanization</u>. Intractable Conflict Knowledge Base Project: University of Colorado: Conflict Research Consortium.

Michael, T. A (n.d.). How to Scapegoat the Leader: A Refresher course (for those who do not need it). <u>Retrieved June 6, 2004, http://www.ipso.org/Symposia/</u> <u>Melbourne/Michael.htm</u>

Milgram, S. (1961). Nationality and conformity; with a biographical sketch. Scientific American, 205(34), 45-51.

O'Toole, K. (1997, January). The Stanford prison experiment: Still powerful after all these years. Stanford University News Service.

Pettigrew, T. F. (1999). Gordon Willard Allport: A tribute. Journal of Social Issues.

Pogonowski, I. C. (n.d.) The German Dehumanizing Routine. Polonia Media Network. Retrieved June 1, 2004, from http://www.poloniatoday.com/pogonowski0303.htm

Preuss, N., Conrad, M., & Wildfeuer, F. (Producers). (2000). The experiment [Motion picture]. (Available from Samuel Goldwyn Films and Senator Film, 10202 W. Washington Blvd., Culver City, CA 90232

Schlabach, J. (1998). In-group, Out-group bias. Living in a Social World – Psy 324: Advanced Social Psychology.

Staub, E. (1989). The roots of evil: The origins of genocide and other group violence. Cambridge, United Kingdom: Cambridge University Press.

Staub, E. (2004). The route to prisoner abuse in Iraq. Monitor on Psychology, 35(7), 9.

The Eternal Jew: The film of a 2000-year rat migration. (1940). Unser Wille and Weg, 10, 54-55.

The Milgram experiment: A lesson in depravity, peer pressure, and the power of authority. (n.d.). Retrieved June 12, 2004, from http://www.new-life.net/milgram.htm

Whiting, C. (2000). The battle for the German frontier. Brooklyn, N.Y: Interlink Books.

Zimbardo, P.G. (1999-2004). Stanford prison experiment: A simulation study of the psychology of imprisonment conducted at Stanford University (slide show). Retrieved June 1, 2004 from http://www.prisonexp.org.

CHAPTER 8
RETOOLING MY LIFE AND PRACTICE FOLLOWING ARMY DEPLOYMENT

"Everybody stop and look at this man." Part the seas and say, "This is your veteran coming home from serving his country. But nobody cared. Nobody gave a goddamn. Nobody gave a damn at all. Nobody." (Brinkley, 2004, p. 329)

The end of my year tour in Germany (i.e. March 2005) was one I had looked forward to from almost the time I first stepped foot on German soil. Being back with my fiancé and kids was a reunion I had rehearsed over and over again. Waiting for the inevitable day to arrive seemed to draw closer, inch by inch, at a very slow pace. So much of my personal and professional life had been placed in a holding pattern during this year long deployment. It thus came as a welcome shot of new life to get on the plane in Frankfurt and head to Ft. Benning, Georgia for out-processing.

A few days before leaving Germany, I wrote a brief e-mail to Judy. *"It was nice to talk to you today. I am getting increasingly excited, as it is becoming obvious the time is drawing near. It takes awhile for this to sink in with me – that tonight will be the last night spent in my apartment, and that Saturday I sky up out of Germany. Even though there will still be a few steps left before I actually get to see you, getting back*

98

onto U.S. soil will be a big psychological step forward…I love you immensely and am feeling your presence increasingly by the moment."

The day of my departure, I hurried off my last communiqué by noting: *"The moment has now arrived. This will be my last e-mail to you from Germany. I am now about to check out of my office here for the last time. Once I walk out, I cannot get back in, as I no longer have a key. I love you beyond measure and can't wait to see you. I will try to call you again before leaving here now."*

In record time, I managed to go through all the clearing stations at Ft. Benning in three days. It was a great feeling to fly out of Columbia, Georgia a "free agent" once again. It struck me how incredibly sudden the transition was from active duty status to the regular Reserve ranks. Even a year of regulated life had left me marveling at the spectacular horizon that now lay in front of me – a renewed life where decision making, options, and contact with family was back in my court.

As big as life, Judy was waiting for me when I came through the doors to baggage claim at the Huntington Airport. It was an emotional and celebratory moment for both of us. We savored as best as we could this memorable moment that ushered in a new chapter. The year of separation had finally come to a close, and we were now able to resume our relationship in close proximity to each other.

My return was a quiet and uneventful event. There was not a welcoming party awaiting my entry into Paintsville. I was simply a lone soldier slipping back into normal society, wearing civilian attire. In my mind, it somehow did not seem fitting for me to be honored publicly like some kind of hero. After all, it is not like I ended up being directly engaged in a combat environment like Iraq or Afghanistan. I was simply providing services for soldiers returning from the fight, safely ensconced in the rear where I labored under a normal work week and traveled around Europe on the weekends.

But, had I been returning from the fight in the Middle East, I am not so sure my silent reentry would have been much different. What significance was there for a community to recognize one soldier coming home, especially when this was not one's original homestead. Had I left and returned with a Reserve unit familiar to the local population, the reception would have likely been prominent and laudatory.

If the worst part of my return was this sense of anonymity, I probably would have carried on with my life with minimal scars. However, when it became apparent that other unpleasant "curve balls" were coming hard at me, my capacity to maintain an optimistic outlook - maintaining faith in the goodwill of others – came under a serious assault. Simply put, there was no way I could have anticipated a returning soldier, especially one with an established profession like mine, could be so disregarded by others in the "know" – ones capable of making a difference. It brought home how alone I really was, aside from my fiancé, family and friends.

The income I had been receiving from the Army came to a screeching halt the very day I went off active duty status. There was not any transition pay to allow for some time to reinvigorate my private practice. None of my previous contracts were now in place, except for the ten hour a week one from the prison. No one was obligated to take me back under federal law, since I was not a regular employee (i.e. contract status). Government responsibility for my financial stability was extinguished as suddenly as it had been initiated a year earlier.

Prior to deployment, my practice included a contract with a private prison, two hospitals, and a supervisory contract with

University of Kentucky. The one hospital in particular had been a substantial piece of my practice. I had worked in the inpatient psychiatric section two days a week for about a year. My affiliation with the hospital went back to my internship there in 1996-1997.

I had hoped the contractual arrangement with this hospital could be renewed upon my return from the Army. A number of the staff had given me high marks for professional competence, and several of them had expressed genuine sorrow to see me leave for a year. My confidence was thus riding pretty high that this solid connection would greatly help facilitate a new contract, especially in light of the circumstances surrounding my departure a year earlier.

It therefore came as quite a shock that the winds had shifted during my absence. Employing psychologists on a part-time contractual basis had fallen into disfavor with the current administration. Despite chronic shortages with psychologists and other mental health staff, the latest view appeared to be inclined toward the hiring of permanent regular employees only.

The visit I scheduled with the director of the psychiatric facility was brief and to the point. My previous internship in this very facility some nine years earlier, the year of contractual work provided just prior to the Army deployment, the quality of my work as a psychologist within this very establishment, and my recent military service all carried little weight in this five minute exchange. His sympathies notwithstanding, the bottom line was that such contractual work no longer existed. That was the end of it and there was no "wiggle room." I left the meeting somewhat in shock and with a sense of disillusionment.

The first step in getting back on track with the other hospital was to regain a credentialed status. This appeared to be a simple enough proposition, since I had been credentialed prior to my deployment for a significant period of time. I was a known quantity, especially with the behavioral health units specializing in an older adult population.

My fate however rested with an out-of-state management group which had secured a contract with the hospital. This group had been assigned responsibility for managing the behavioral health units, both inpatient and outpatient. Furthermore, one particular point person had tremendous influence in determining how things were administered.

I had consulted with this individual a few times prior to the deployment. He encouraged me to brainstorm with him about possible directions the hospital might go with regard to the behavioral health units. We talked about such things as a psychologist conducting direct service within the hospital, mental health coverage in the emergency room and employee assistance programs. It had actually been very refreshing to talk with such a seemingly "free-spirited" management person about many of the aspirations I personally held for the direction of the hospital and the region as a whole (i.e. in terms of mental health issues and potential programs).

It was with considerable optimism that I met with this imaginative entrepreneur again over breakfast to discuss ways I could supplement existing behavioral health services. My idea of providing clinical services within the hospital to patients being referred by physicians seemed to meet his approval. The director of the outpatient unit at the hospital was present also, and she gave supportive input for how much my services were needed. In exchange for psychological coverage of hospital referrals, I would be granted office space and an established infrastructure. I would initiate my own billing and would work closely with the in-house psychiatrist. The informal meeting ended on a positive note, and I was heartily welcomed back from military service.

Since this peak experience, attempt after attempt of reaching this man had failed. The director of the outpatient program continually encouraged me to get a hold of him directly, and my complaints of his unresponsiveness were met with further entreaties to try even harder. The representative for this management group had seemed to acquire such illusive abilities that I could not catch him in the midst of his pursuit for deals and opportunities covering several states. The outpatient director sympathized with my laments and growing perception that dealing with the hospital directly was the preferred course.

In exasperation, and after consultation with the director, I submitted for credentialing separate from my connection to this management group. Finally, after nearly a year of waiting, I gained the coveted credentialed status. The remaining problem was that any work I did at the hospital still needed to be coordinated by this management group that even the outpatient director had difficulties clarifying with them.

More recently, the outpatient program for older adults had closed, and the director who had been so supportive of securing me a place at the hospital had moved on as well. The program had proved to be too much of a fiscal liability for the hospital, and had been governed by a management group that seemed to be quite remote.

I cannot help but have some resentment toward this management individual who so flagrantly provided false hopes of an agreement just around the corner. He kept stringing me along by leaving messages with the outpatient director that I should call him, or that we should meet. Worst of all was his engagement in such avoidant behavior with full knowledge of the sacrifice I had made in serving the country we both were a part of. He was clearly aware of my predicament in getting my private practice reestablished, and how much I could benefit by securing an agreement for office space. Yet, he failed to follow through with any actions beyond apparent indifference, and most gallingly without any explanation.

One day in the spring I showed up at the Veterans Administration in Huntington to obtain a temperature read on employment possibilities. There were several staff who showed considerable interest in a psychologist like me with prior military experience and immediate availability for contractual work. They encouraged me to follow-up this initial visit with a phone call to the psychologist in charge of the behavioral health unit.

Their enthusiastic reception bolstered my confidence that the need existed for a psychologist to provide some assessment services. My optimism was short lived following a discussion with the head psychologist. Having come out of a graduate school program and internship - one certified by the American Psychological Association (APA) only after my completion – placed me in a precarious position with regard to hiring. She informed me of her uncertainty whether a waiver from the normal requirement for APA approved status would make a difference.

Having previously obtained a waiver under the same federal requirement for Army Reserve duty as a psychologist, this having been a cumbersome three to four year process, did not appear to change anything. She admitted her unfamiliarity with the process of seeking a waiver, and seemed disinclined to expend too much energy toward such an end. This was apparent even though my offer for contractual work came at a time when VA was experiencing some mental health manpower shortages.

Despite her agreement to look further into the waiver process, further communication proved to be more of the same – no breakthroughs as yet. Eventually, my phone calls produced no reciprocating return calls at all. What appeared to be a rather good fit turned out to have some governmental tangles that even very recent military service could not unravel. My specialized experience with military personnel turned out to be non-transferable to the organization with the single largest collection of individuals previously associated with the armed forces, many in dire need of quality psychological services.

Another quagmire with a different set of issues emerged when I attempted to seek contractual employment with various military installations. Initially I contacted the behavioral health units at Fort Knox and Fort Campbell in Kentucky. Ultimately, probes were made with out of state Army sites as far afield as Ft. Bragg, North Carolina and Fort Carson, Colorado.

Despite a need for psychological services of returning soldiers from Iraq and Afghanistan, as well as with family members, there appeared to be insurmountable red tape involved which exceeded my capacity to pursue indefinitely. I could not hang around in limbo while the Army sorted out how to allocate appropriate levels of care for its own, and determine whether Reserve mental health types should be incorporated into their response to the burgeoning demand.

The most appalling situation I became aware of was with Fort Knox, the Army post closest to my residence. The behavioral health unit was not in a position itself to authorize a contractual agreement. This went through an office in the hospital which specifically handled contracts. The individual I spoke with matter of factly informed me   psychological assessment and therapy was being "farmed out" to Tricare (i.e. the health care insurance entity for military personnel).

I could not maintain an entirely professional demeanor, as I expressed my utter shock and disappointment that soldiers, spouses and children traumatized by the war had to seek out services with off-post providers who were civilians with varying levels of knowledge and expertise in working with a "military culture." Even if adequate competency existed with providers, I knew that many soldiers would be disinclined to "open up" in therapy with a professional who was not directly connected to the Army, both from a positional standpoint and an emotional one.

My experience in Baumholder, Germany had taught me the importance of providing psychological services in close proximity to the units and living quarters where the soldiers, spouses and children resided. Many with significant psychological difficulties were much more likely to seek out services close to home. As had been impressed upon me, this likelihood was further enhanced when individuals were referred, and even introduced, from their Army physician who was physically near the mental health provider's office. This of course was ideal, and even when both the physical and behavioral health issues get addressed on a military installation, treating physicians and behavioral health providers may be separated by different floors of a hospital, or different parts of the Army post altogether.

The Tricare approach struck me as a system of care which would effectively prevent a significant number of soldiers and families from accessing the psychological services needed. In my judgment, this would occur not because independent providers were unavailable, but rather because too many psychological barriers would crop up in the minds of the intended recipients of Tricare. The combined negative impact of distance from home, lack of direct connection with the treating physician, discomfort with non-military providers, and internal ambivalence regarding treatment for psychological problems to begin with, helped explain how an unsuccessful physician or self-referral could occur.

Even if an individual made it successfully for the first session with a Tricare provider, cognitive dissonance would likely be riding high. Even a seasoned and skilled clinician would be hard pressed to establish the kind of rapport and understanding of what the individual had been through to keep him or her coming back and really engaging in therapy.

My only sliver of sunshine was the prison position that was being handed back to me. The mental health therapist who had filled in for me in the previous year had been asked to discontinue her services in order to allow my return. I was very relieved the prison had kept their promise made just prior to my year deployment.

Their commitment to me was short lived when two months later the prison was completely shut down. Their contract to house out of state inmates had expired, and the inmates returned to newly established prison space in their home state. My only viable source of income had abruptly fizzled, placing me in as desperate a state financially I had been in over twenty years of steady employment.

There was no way I could "stay afloat" from the meager payments trickling in from the few clients being seen out of my private office. For the first time since my undergraduate days in the 70's, I submitted a computerized claim with the unemployment office. My case was viewed as being quite unique because of my educational level and previous work experience. This was particularly true when they considered my private practice previously operative, and the one officially "open for business" since coming off active duty.

Despite the efforts of a sympathetic staff person at the Unemployment office who specialized with returning soldiers, I never did receive any compensation for the several weeks of extremely limited income. I chose to focus on reestablishing business however I could rather than expend any more energy clawing after governmental assistance. This whole episode had been humiliating to say the least, and once again reinforced the realization that I was truly on my own.

Compounding my financial woes, I had made a commitment while still in Germany to conduct a presentation on my work with soldiers and spouses. This was set to occur a few months after my release from active duty in the Bavarian region of Germany very close to the Austrian border – an area particularly scenic because of the German-Austrian Alps at your doorstep and the lushness of the surrounding vegetation. A sprawling hotel in the town of Sonthofen had been reserved as the site for this week long Army Medical conference.

I thought for sure the Army would pick up the tab for my travel to the conference. To my chagrin, I was informed that no funding could be provided for travel or rental car because the conference was outside the continental United States. Had the conference been located anywhere in the contiguous 48 states, my travel expenses would have been covered. As with the other invited participants and speakers, the hotel and food expenses were paid for by the Army.

My decision to attend regardless was based on my conviction that my presentation would be helpful for those attending. It was also a chance for my fiancé to be a part of a military event she had been unable to during my year in Germany. It turned out that I co-presented with another psychologist who had been in Iraq. He took the first half hour to talk about mental health issues in a combat environment. I then focused on clinical issues with soldiers returning from Iraq and Afghanistan, as well as their spouses who had resided in Germany during the "down-range" deployment.

This return trip to Germany also helped me in reconnecting once more with some of the military persons I had worked with at Landstuhl Regional Hospital. This included my former boss and his wife. It simply had not been an easy task to disengage from the level of responsibility and mission previously assigned to me. I had grown fond of the group of mental health professionals I worked with, and had experienced more of a sense of loss and connection with them than had been anticipated. The conference served to soften my landing back to the civilian world. It helped to extend my time of commitment and service just a bit longer.

Since the Army would not finance my airfare to Germany, I tried another route with a congressman in the state. A veterans group had indicated that congressional staff could access special funds often available for requests like mine. When a phone call with an explanation did not produce any results, I delivered a typed statement of my request for financial support at the main office. Even a year later, there still had not been any feedback from any staff person out of this congressman's office. Even a negative response would have been better than a protracted silence like this.

Between the months of March and May 2005, I provided presentations to two Rotary Clubs and one Kiwanis Club. A liaison person at the local community college became interested in my work with soldiers and spouses in Germany. She arranged for these three presentations, making it so much easier to access these community groups.

On the face of it, these presentations were rather straight forward and uncomplicated. It simply involved a recap and condensed version of the formal presentation done in Sonthofen, Germany. What took me by surprise were some of the reactions by some attending who had prior service experience, sometimes dating back to World War II or the Korean War. It was reaffirming to hear them talk about these earlier experiences, relating to some of the psychological issues addressed in my presentation. I was profoundly humbled that a current explication of psychological factors related to Operation Iraqi Freedom could reignite the buried memories of seemingly ancient wars and elicit such passionate recollections.

Another source of income I attempted to reclaim was doing guardianship evaluations – ones determining whether elderly persons were sufficiently intact cognitively and mentally to manage their own affairs. I did a number of these prior to the Germany deployment and felt confident that local judges would want to send some of these evaluations my way again.

Officials connected with a nearby county court were contacted. They expressed their support of my proposal and welcomed me back. All I had to do was approach one of the judges who had been instrumental in sending out evaluation requests to select providers. Following several failed attempts to reach him by phone or in his office, I finally managed to set up a meeting with him. He indicated a willingness to provide me some business and expressed approval of my guardianship fees. I parted with an understanding that he would start to send me referrals in the near future.

In my delight at renewing some "old business," I forwarded an e-mail to the judge noting my contact with court officials in a neighboring county. It read, *"It was good to talk with you the other day. Your suggestions on how to proceed with 'Guardianship Evaluations' was very helpful. Also, I found it very interesting to hear how things work with 'Drug Court' and court referrals for treatment.*

I did consult with _____________ about doing guardianships. He was very supportive of the idea. He indicated that the 'Fiscal Court' handles the payment part, but it was his belief that reimbursement for services was being pushed through fairly rapidly.

I also consulted with __________ who handles the guardianship paperwork that comes through. She indicated they were fairly backed up due to other commitments by the previous provider…She further stated that all it would take for me to get on board is to receive a 'court order' naming me as a provider of guardianship evaluation services.

I trust the information provided is useful on your end. Your assistance in getting me restarted is appreciated. Please feel free to contact me should further discussion on this subject be desired."

After several months had passed, it became apparent that something had gone awry. I was too deflated by the lack of response to pursue the guardianship proposal any further. It has remained puzzling since then what sequence of events brought this opportunity to an untimely end.

My fortune took a more positive turn by June 2005 when an attorney hired me for a very involved and complex forensic case. This occurred during a period when I was not getting much business, following the loss of my prison contract. I welcomed the opportunity to work on a new project and to feel, once again, that my skills were being put to good use. It could not have come at a better time in terms of revitalizing my practice and my rather tattered spirit.

Even before my year in Germany, I harbored an interest in working in a long-term care facility (i.e. nursing home). My busy schedule and uncertainty of how viable such work would be kept me from actually getting started. Yet, I clearly recognized the need for psychologists to be involved since many of these facilities were without any mental health services.

In June 2005, the time seemed right to give the long-term care facility a try. There were a number of housekeeping matters to clear up. So, the input of qualified mental health professionals working in nursing homes in the state were sought after. The feedback I did receive helped to prepare myself for some of the institutional and patient related challenges inherent to this population.

After getting some new forms generated specific to a geriatric group of people, as well as a thorough review of APA guidelines, I started to conduct individual sessions with residents and billing directly to Medicare and Medicaid. In time my awareness increased dramatically regarding the difficulty of seeing very many residents in a day. I also became painfully aware of the poor reimbursement rate allotted to me by Medicare. The meager financial return made it difficult to justify the time invested in tracking down patients who actually wanted to be seen.

Still, the residents grew on me in ways quite unexpected. Some of them definitely displayed an enormous need for someone neutral to talk with, and helped me to engage them in a more meaningful manner.

It came as some surprise that a connection emerged between nursing home residents and soldiers/spouses in the military. In both cases, death and dying issues were very prominent, weighing heavily on people's minds. Instead of getting away from the "angel of death" scenario in the military, my work at the nursing home thrust me even further into the essential struggle existing between life and death. I could not get away from the reality that several residents on my caseload had suddenly died, often without much warning.

The rest of the summer proved to be quite lean. But, I did not want to deprive my kids of another summer without contact with relatives on the west coast. Disliking the idea of going into debt, the trip was nevertheless financed with a credit card. It was really meaningful to see my two brothers and their families, along with my mother. My fiancé came to

Twisp, Washington with me, this being a good time for her to be welcomed into the family – marriage just being around the corner.

My mission to speak out about my experiences in Germany still had not run its course out of my veins. It had thus been arranged in advance I would speak at the local church my mother belonged to, the topic being on my work with soldiers and spouses. Two of my high school buddies happened to come out to visit during this time frame. In addition my two brothers and some of their family members were also present. I felt embarrassed and quite awkward to be giving a serious presentation with friends and family in the audience. I certainly did not want to leave the impression I was "grandstanding" in front of them.

I'm assuming the presentation went rather well, given the positive feedback. It was obvious these individuals from a small community in a hot and sparsely populated area of Eastern Washington had a profound interest in the psychological impact on soldiers and spouses. Several attendees approached me during the reception afterward to talk about their concerns regarding the war. It became apparent to me that my presentation triggered a number of visceral responses that had already been simmering. Even though this presentation had been neutral on the politics surrounding the war in Iraq, it seemed to act as a springboard for the whole range of perspectives various people held about U.S. involvement in the war.

The question once again confronted me. Why was I still offering basically the same presentation about my work with soldiers and spouses some six months following my return from Germany? It appeared pretty straight forward on the surface. I considered it important for regular citizens to be better informed about psychological factors of the war. Also, especially in light of my financial woes, I was trying to move toward a place of public speaking that would include some remuneration. But, was that really what was driving the engine here?

Admittedly, a more fundamental issue was "worming" its way through my system. There had been so much of my experience in Germany that I had not fully dealt with as yet. The things I heard from soldiers and spouses, and the many demands placed on me to shoulder their struggles, had all taken much more of a toll on me than I could have ever realized at any given point.

It had become more apparent in the ensuing months following my return that I had some unresolved anger about the things I saw and experienced in Germany. I had become privy to the many ways in the midst of prosecuting a war that individual soldiers and their families had suffered beyond what was necessary.

So many different situations had been communicated to me during therapy sessions of insensitive, degrading and cruel actions within the ranks of our own military and the chain of command. Then, there were all the shocking stories coming back from the front pertaining to the maiming and destruction of human life, whether that be with American soldiers, insurgents or Iraqi citizens with varying degrees of innocence. As with many other soldiers, I was doing battle within myself regarding the ultimate price being paid by so many for reasons that seemed to lack the kind of justification that satisfies a questioning mind like mine. My accumulated frustration had also mounted in response to the blocking of my own study of the Abu Ghraib scandal, and what a blow this had been to my core beliefs about the type of society I was a part of.

I simply could not go back to civilian life and leave all that I knew and had experienced behind. There was too much at stake, too many lives still hanging in the balance, to be able to pull off a clean break. I had been afflicted with the same kind of self-assumed obligation that many soldiers had encountered – that surging need to return to the combat zone and complete what was still only in process.

But, in my case, I felt compelled to immerse myself deeply in the essential humanity issues which the war had spawned. I wanted to uncover how we as a civilized culture had reached this point of unleashing a war fervor that feeds on itself like an inexhaustible and furious inferno, and one where the single solution appears to be the annihilation of the identified enemy. I felt a desperate need to reach beyond the limits of our finite minds, as in the quest to actually encounter the godhead, in order to discover the hidden nuggets in the universe which guide us beyond the human drive to literally incinerate groups of people we are at odds with.

My experience of this war has left me with such dissatisfaction for conventional patriotism, soldierly bravado, and determination to carry out the mission regardless of the human costs. In its place, I am afflicted with a wrenching wound in my soul that cannot be appeased. The level of human suffering that has occurred in this war by all involved parties is staggering and impossible deep within me to keep my distance from. Perhaps adequate reasons are never forthcoming for those confronted with the consequences of war, as with an Iraqi mother holding the mangled body of her beloved child in her arms or an American soldier cradling the stilled body of a comrade he or she had grown so profoundly fond of. And here I am, just a soldier specialized in the grandeur of the human mind and emotions, gazing from the sidelines at the human wreckage all about, and unable to loosen my fixed stare from the shock of what is, and the disturbing thought of what could have been.

The anger therefore cropped up in unexpected spasms, sometimes when I attempted to sort through my emotions with my fiancé. How could I begin to articulate in a controlled manner the anguish of the war that had entered my own being, and could not be sufficiently assuaged. Even as a trained psychologist, I lacked the resources to communicate the kind of struggle I was facing, especially when my own awareness of this affliction was limited and for a time denied.

It took the two of us sitting across from a private practice psychologist to begin the process of dredging out the array of emotions tangled up with my experience of the war in Germany. What until then had been a kind of unintelligible spraying around of intense feelings became in time a more coherent picture of a soldier deeply impacted by a war with so many disturbing facets. I had to come to terms with my own humanity, that I was not able to objectively soak in all that soldiers and spouses had confided to me about their experiences and remain untouched.

Just a month before our marriage in September, the prison came to new life. This time it had been transformed into a women's prison and everyone involved was on a similar learning curve. The previous contract I had enjoyed just a few months earlier before the prison closed for the summer months was now null and void. Furthermore, it was uncertain at best whether I would even be included under the new system. The management had changed considerably, and some of the former staff were not asked to return.

The invitation came for me to accept a full-time position at the prison. Assuming such a role would have made it difficult for me to maintain a varied practice. My freedom as a private practice provider would have likewise been terminated, and I would then have been subjected to the regular employee requirements to include limitations on vacation. It would have been a throw back to a year and a half before my deployment to Germany when I left a community mental health center for private practice. I was not ready to submit to such a fate as yet.

When the prison officials clearly understood my resolve, I was asked to submit a proposal outlining among other things the hours I could perform weekly and the hourly pay. I had been advised ahead of time that they would not be able to pay me the same rates as before. Based on this, I submitted a proposal that called for considerably less money than what I had always received in the past. My proposal was rejected outright. It looked as if they were trying to hire a full-time psychologist at a much reduced rate.

The prison opened around the middle of August 2005, and they still had not landed a psychologist. So, in their desperation, I was asked to provide some temporary services until they could hire someone. They informed me that they had someone in mind, and that it would be just a matter of weeks before this person took over. Several weeks went by while I worked at my previous pay rate.

It started to occur to me that their psychologist in the wings was not going to materialize. This eventually led to a request for me to come up with an hourly rate lower than my previous one. Desperate for a secured contract, I offered a further reduction in hourly fees. An agreement was thus forged. Some six months after my return from Germany, the first major contract was reestablished. Although glad to be gainfully employed with a steady number of weekly hours, it panged me to have been in such a weakened state that a substantial reduction had become palatable.

Any fantasies I had entertained regarding the prison taking me back under similar circumstances prior to deployment vanished in the settlement that was reached. My previous service in Germany appeared to bear little influence on the negotiations and outcome of the contract.

Just over a month following the new contract with the prison, my fiancé and I flew to Maui for two weeks of relaxation. But, the highlight of the trip - the real reason for going - was our marriage on the sandy beach in front of our hotel. The rain had poured for a time just prior to our special occasion. Barefoot, we took our vows with a setting sun covered over by clouds. It was close to what we both imagined it would look like. We were grateful to have timed it right between rain showers and to have experienced the grandeur and splash of vivid colors of the widely romanticized sunsets along this slice of the Maui shoreline.

My own "demons" from the war had not left me completely. There were still plenty of internal conflicts and unsettledness to be sifted out, as this book has attested to. Still, I had reached a kind of plateau where the slog was not so daunting, and one where I felt ready to move on with the woman I loved. In the midst of all the destruction and human loss, I had found a way to reopen my heart to another more unaffected by the droning drumbeats promoting ongoing hostilities, and find at least temporarily a sanctuary seemingly a million miles away from the conflagration.

On two more occasions in the Fall months, I felt compelled to present on my work with soldiers and spouses in Germany. Some of the psychology students at Transylvania University, as well as faculty members, heard my presentation in October 2005. This was followed by a final presentation at the Kentucky Psychological Association in November.

I somehow knew this would likely be the last time I would publicly speak on the topic. It had been important for me to inform civilian audiences about the struggles of soldiers and spouses within my sphere of involvement, from a vantage point of personal experience. The drive to ascend the "soapbox" anymore after the KPA convention just did not feel right. Every one of my presentations had its share of personal challenges. I no longer felt capable of dealing with the pain brought on by reliving the trauma of so many of those I had worked with. Any further renditions of my psychological work there would have seemed artificial, contrived and lacking in intensity what these men and women deserved. Speaking out too much on a particular topic has limitations and breaking points culminating in "burn out." This is at least how it ran its course with me.

All in all, the first six months back were very nerve-wracking. There were not any jobs or contracts which were handed to me easily. Everything seemed to call for strenuous effort on my part. I could not even rely on the military establishment itself to facilitate a position for me.

What has occurred to me since is that so many other solders have likely gone down a similar road where they were virtually forgotten once discharged from military duty. Treatment like this has to play on a soldier's mind, perhaps influencing their own perseverance to obtaining a job and reestablishing a productive life on the outside.

I consider myself fortunate in that my professional skills were not thwarted for too long. My ability to eventually secure work was high, since it was just a matter of time before contracts and clients would come my way. Even so, the road was pretty bumpy for a time, and I would have felt particularly relieved if someone would have offered a helping hand.

References
Brinkley, D. (2004). <u>Tour of duty</u>. New York:
Harper Collins Publishers

CHAPTER 9
AN ARMY CAREER HANGING IN THE BALANCE

No one is arguing for active duty insubordination. Officers who cannot support the policy they are called upon to carry out should resign. Few do. Some are deterred by post-retirement employment considerations. Many refuse this option because they consider it tantamount to abandoning troops in the field. Others know that influence evanesces once you step down. And others don't do it because it's rarely been done.

Now we are seeing the beginnings of a possibility that transcends protest: the chance for such officers to educate the American people. And if this is happening, it may be just another sign of the military reconnecting with American culture and society in some very unexpected ways (Solaro, 2006, p. 2).

It was not long after my return from Germany that I found myself struggling to maintain an interest in the military. Other than my return trip to the medical/behavioral health conference in Sonthofen, Germany, the thought of doing any Reserve training was rather an anathema. I truthfully found myself lacking in motivation to pursue any annual training, military related conferences, or anything with a semblance of connection to the armed forces. The idea of donning my

120

camouflage uniform, lacing up my combat boots and putting on my black beret was far from appealing. Quite simply, I wanted to keep the Army regalia in the closet and carry on with my life as if I was completely free from any further military obligations.

The last time I harbored such strong sentiments was when I was discharged from three years of active duty in 1976. When the commanding officer of my battalion in South Korea tried to talk me into reenlisting, I confidently asserted that I was getting out in order to pursue a college education. What I did not tell this Lieutenant Colonel was that my ultimate reason for getting out was to escape a lifestyle completely at odds with who I was, and where I wanted to go. I did not want to disappoint my commanding officer with the reality that his training NCO had determined that further military service was particularly noxious to even contemplate.

Back then, three years of active Army experience with both infantry and airborne units had given me my fill of Army life. I had been exposed to a number of Vietnam stories by soldiers who had been there and, despite it all, had decided to stay in. There were also the many career soldiers, officer and enlisted alike, who were convinced that their best bet for job security was to remain with the Army. The compilation of these views helped to solidify a determination that I was not going to be caught up like some of them in the military trappings which would mentally foster dependency on a military paycheck, quarters and the mess hall.

I have often spoken of a love/hate relationship with the military that never could be resolved. While expanding one's horizons with free travel and potential overseas assignments, there was also the reality that once arrived at a duty station one had to cope with the monotony of being fixed to one place and job function. Making changes on the spur of the moment, or even more methodically, was extremely difficult to achieve – the end result being a sense of "stuck-ness" with tasks and certain undesirable individuals to contend with. Those who were in it for the long haul had learned the art of "riding out" a miserable assignment until being reassigned some three or four years "down the road."

Then there were the issues with rank, and the multitude of problems which cropped up in dealing with soldiers of superior rank. There was the monumental task of controlling one's behavior when dealing with a higher ranking NCO or officer, most troublesome when the ranking individual abused their position of authority. Holding back one's anger and defensive responses in the face of such inane verbal denunciations and "power tripping" certainly took its toll over time.

Shortly after being assigned to Battalion headquarters with the 82nd Airborne Division in 1973, my capacities for self-control were sorely challenged. A Captain in the administrative arm of headquarters approached me. He quickly pointed out how sloppy my uniform looked. He then proceeded to pull out my shirt with the idea of demonstrating the correct way of tucking the fatigue top into my pants. It took everything I could muster to avoid slapping away his hands as he was manually loosening my belt buckle and shoving the shirt into my pants. I remember being struck by his rather transparent attempt to humiliate by taking control over me with such a basic and personal task.

Not far from my mind when signing my discharge papers at Fort Lewis in 1976 was the thought of coming to an end of the Army "red tape" and the whole bureaucratic morass which had so engulfed me. No longer would I have to deal with endless waiting while being channeled through various stations, whether this be in-processing, out-processing, cleaning weapons or gas masks, dealing with financial pay issues, clearing one's military vehicle at the motor pool, and a huge array of other seemingly simple functions made frustratingly difficult. This endless stream of paperwork and tedious tasks designed for large groups of soldiers would finally come to a close, and none too soon.

This being said, the reasons for my mental defection so many years later was rooted in an entirely different set of issues. I was no longer grumbling about the rank issues, the bureaucracy, or the quality of the assignments per se. Certainly all of these could be very annoying at times, but years of maturation within the military system had enabled me to adapt to these aspects of Army life.

Now the issues were directed at the larger picture of an "ugly war" being prosecuted for dubious reasons. I was now contending with fundamental philosophical views of life and treatment of others, including the targeted enemy. I found myself questioning whether my values were so different from the U.S. military's, as manifested in this war, that my retirement was no longer debatable.

How could I possibly consider remaining within the Reserve ranks when "breakouts of inhumanity" from American soldiers were occurring with apparent greater frequency, and with very inadequate mechanisms built in the system to investigate and prosecute all those responsible for wrongdoing without regard to rank? Had not the Army's refusal to allow publication of the "Abu Ghraib" paper opened my eyes wide enough to see the level of resistance to genuine inquiry into actions taken by military personnel? Was it not the case that my excessively naïve beliefs of promoting a more humane and compassionate military really been "dashed on the rocks" in the face of the reality of what was happening on the ground in Iraq and Afghanistan?

In an attempt to publish articles following a return to Reserve status, my interactions with scholarly organizations affiliated with the military proved to further undermine my faith in such institutions and the military establishment as a whole. It seemed quite apparent these journals were screening for articles sympathetic to the "party line" within the military.

Among the several journals I sent manuscripts to, there was one in particular recommended to me which clearly displayed such a bias. I initiated contact with the following e-mail. *"I have a paper ready for submission to the appropriate journal. It involves a psychological study of the Abu Ghraib prisoner abuse situation, utilizing four different theories or research studies. It is quite readable for a generalist population and is about 20 pages long. The paper is partly experiential and partially focused on the theories. There are a good number of references.*

The paper was written last summer while I was still on active duty in Germany. I am currently back to the civilian world, although still in the Army Reserve.

Does this paper sound like a possible 'good fit' for______ ______? Please advise." In what seemed to be record time, the managing editor e-mailed me back with a verdict. He wrote, *"We appreciated the opportunity to consider your manuscript 'Abu Ghraib: A Psychological Search for How Such Dehumanization of Detainees Could Occur,' but we will not be able to publish it in ___________. Despite the merits of your work, we are unable to accept it for our journal given the current needs, our space constraints, and the number of manuscripts we are presently receiving."*

I decided to try another article with the same journal. The e-mail read, *"Your timely response regarding the Abu Ghraib paper I submitted is appreciated. Even though it did not work out with ___________, I was glad to get your feedback so quickly. This helped me to resubmit it to another journal in short order.*

There is another paper I wrote while in Germany that may be of interest to you and the reviewers at ___________. Please find the cover letter attached to this e-mail."

This managing editor of the journal quickly responded the same day. He wrote, *"The paper you outline in your letter is indeed one that we would like to consider. A couple of cautions: Our readers are generalists, so the manuscript would have to be accessible to them, not overly clinical in content or language. Also, you would need to guard against presenting only the negative, if there are any positives to report.*

A manuscript built on the psychological impact of combat in Iraq on soldiers and their families is something we would like to publish, assuming of course that the manuscript is well executed and garners the approval of our referees."

I was already sensing that this second manuscript might also have troubles being approved. The editor appeared to be narrowing the field of what was acceptable. Of course, he had already turned down one of my articles that fell outside the range they were looking for.

Sure enough, four days after I sent the manuscript on working with soldiers and spouses in Germany, the managing editor e-mailed back their decision. He wrote, *"We appreciated the opportunity to consider your manuscript 'Personal Reflections on War, Death, and the Act of Living,' but we will not be able to publish it in ___________. As the title suggests, it's too much in the vein of 'personal reflections' to be publishable in an academic journal such as ours."*

It was very deflating to not get it right according to their specifications two times in a row. Yes, it could be argued that my writing style and readability were not up to standards. Still, this factor alone should have led to some proposed revisions rather than a cursory rejection. The reference the editor made regarding the need for "positive content" perhaps revealed more centrally the crux of the problem. Thus a reasonable counter hypothesis could be proposed that the articles appeared too critical or questioning of the military which could then be thought as too offensive to their readership.

The free speech issue which I had personally been compelled to contend with also loomed large on the landscape. Being in the Reserve did not afford one the same level of open and unfettered communication that was a constitutional right of the typical citizen. Possession of the military identification card brought one special privileges like shopping at the PX or the commissary. It also ushered in regulatory expectations of appropriate conduct and communication that would impact the decision making process in any situation. A conscientious soldier had to continually be on "one's toes" about what was conveyed in written and oral form, so as to avoid disciplinary actions.

I had assured my wife that I would consult with an attorney about any possible problems associated with the writing of this book. Contact was made with an attorney who advertised as being a specialist with military law. He advised me to send an e-mail outlining the issues I was concerned about.

I sent the following e-mail. *"Thanks for getting back to me so quickly. I'm assuming that everything I discuss is confidential, as with standard attorney-client privilege. Incidentally, I am more than happy to pay for the time you take to address my concerns. A lot hinges on your assistance and expert advice. I would much prefer you take the necessary time to provide solid counsel.*

I am a CPT in the Army Reserve. Recently, I was involuntarily activated to Germany for a year to work with soldiers and spouses as a clinical psychologist. I wrote some articles while there with the intent of publishing. One was approved, and one was not.

I was informed by my boss that I would have more freedom to publish once released from active duty in March 2005. So, I have been attempting to do this.

Due to the typical difficulties of publishing in a timely way, I have now opted to write a book that highlights several of my papers, including the one turned down for publication while on active duty.

One of the issues the book will address is how the military prevented me from publishing an academic article, along with the feelings I had about that. I am not naming names and not vilifying any superior officers, except noting what my boss actually told me about my proposed article.

I am also highlighting my disagreement with the military stance about 'freedom of speech,' and am indicating my general opposition to the war – again without discrediting any particular leader.

There is a part of me that would like to stay in the military. After all, I now have 23 years Reserve, 4 years active, and 3 years inactive Reserve (IRR). I personally believe the military would be better served to allow for a greater amount of free speech, and I would like to contribute toward such an end.

But, if staying in means the possibility of legal troubles with the military (i.e. UCMJ), I would then resign my commission in order to publish the book unhindered.

So, there it is. I just need to know what is advisable under these circumstances. Any assistance you can provide is very much appreciated."

Although this attorney had initially expressed an interest in reviewing the military matters I alluded to, his response seemed to head in another direction altogether. He wrote: *"This looks interesting but I'm going to have to pass. Unfortunately, I've been busy traveling and wouldn't be able to give your work the attention it needs. Thanks for contacting me."*

One could not help but be puzzled with such an about-face. Was there something inherent to the military law issues I was seeking an opinion on that proved to be disturbing enough to create a "cold feet" syndrome? Was I raising some fundamental questions about freedom of speech issues in the military during a time of war that attorneys might perceive as potentially damaging to their practice and status? Was it possible I was even delving into some sacrosanct territory associated with loyalty to country and flag – sensitive matters that could possibly intimidate legal minds and create fears of being pegged as un-American? These were some of the musings that tumbled through my mind in the wake of this attorney's retreat.

I responded to his e-mail with a request. *"Thanks for your candor. Do you have anyone you could refer me to?"* As I suspected, he did not reply to this appeal for assistance. I would simply have to accept the remaining mystery surrounding this brief, but pregnant, interchange between an attorney and a psychologist.

The very writing of this book produced a powerful argument in favor of getting a full discharge from the Army. In fact, for aspiring writers and critics of military policy, a ubiquitous practice has been to first separate from military service prior to publication of controversial and critical writings about the Army or other branches of service. Even in this present war, we have seen such a pattern emerge, right up to the top brass – retired generals coming forth with their scathing commentaries of military actions and governmental failings.

Solaro (2006) noted in her Post Intelligencer article:

Publicizing his book, "The Battle for Peace," in a recent "Meet the Press" appearance, retired Marine Gen. Anthony Zinni, a four-star former commander of the Central

Command, describes administration behavior that ranged from "true dereliction, negligence and irresponsibility" to "lying, incompetence and corruption." Another Marine, retired Lt. Gen. Greg Newbold, has written in Time magazine that the Iraq war was unnecessary. Finally, Lt. Gen. Bernard Trainor and Michael Gordon have written a history of the invasion of Iraq, Cobra II, which describes a willfully self-deluding planning process (p.1).

Even if philosophical differences could not compel me to resign my commission, my determination to see through the writing of this book served as the ultimate rationale par excellence. The truth of my experience in Germany and in the aftermath of my return needed to be told without frantic attempts to make it palatable for military sensibilities, and without obsessive fears of reprisal.

Getting out made perfectly good sense, as noted by my pragmatic wife and by my own judgment during lucid moments. Taking this large step would free me from the ongoing sense of internal dividedness between military service for country and my humanitarian impulses. I just had to come to terms with the fact that one cannot be a devoted soldier and reflective-critical writer of military matters at the same time.

It all sounded so uncomplicated and reasonable. Yet, the act of picking up the phone and making the call to Reserve headquarters in St. Louis seemed to be so utterly difficult to carry out. It was personally shocking to observe how torn I was with this action. I even purposely pushed it out of my mind, anything to delay an actual decision.

My mind referred back in time to an earlier, more impressionable period as a young paper boy. Day after day, I had to face the same taunting "hoodlum" who knew how to "rub in" my feeling of inadequacy and fearfulness. I must have rehearsed a hundred times the idea of standing up to this guy for better or worse in order to break out of the unbearable tension occurring daily. So, in an existentially pregnant moment forever remembered in panoramic detail, I stepped through the door and challenged him to "have at it." The fight itself was essentially anticlimactic and surprisingly easy on my part. It did not even compare with the actual decision to plant my feet and "prepare for battle."

Here I was again, waffling on something I was so convinced of doing while still in Germany. Through all the frustrations and agonies of being a Reserve NCO, and later an officer, there remained a kind of marriage to this complex institution that defied logic. Over the years I had grown used to being a rather insignificant "cog" in the Army machinery.

But there had been moments of exhilaration and anticipation of what lay around the next corner. New assignments always had a way of whetting my appetite for a time. I had pinned high hopes on fresh orders to the Pentagon, Panama, Pearl Harbor and Heidelberg, Germany. Even when the novelty wore off and the actual duties became tedious and seemingly unimportant in the larger scheme of things, I could still utilize my free time with sightseeing and explorations of the surrounding culture. Covering new terrain, both figurative and actual, seemed to be the key in keeping me in the ballpark.

Yet, I came to realize the real driving force behind my ongoing military commitment was a sense of incompletion. Analogous to my professional life as a civilian, I was still awaiting the quintessential event or period in the Army where I could accomplish a mission of great significance - one held in high esteem by those in uniform, civilians and myself. The pinnacle of my military career had hardly revealed itself up to now. But it would only be possible to actualize this dream by staying in the Reserves. It remains to be seen whether this current literary endeavor would prove to be the elusive peak sought after for so long.

It was becoming increasingly clear that I was in need of sound advice. I turned to a colleague who had supported me in other publication endeavors, going back to graduate school.

My query to him read, *"I have enclosed an e-mail I sent to an attorney regarding freedom of speech issues in the military. As you can see, he declined to offer an opinion. Even though you are not an attorney, I would still welcome your thoughts about my predicament.*

In addition, with regard to my proposed book, I have a chapter describing my reactions, and communications made, following the Abu Ghraib paper being denied authorization to publish. I would like to include some e-mail correspondence between us, but only if this is alright with you. Believe me, I can understand if you decline. The feedback you provided in the e-mails pertained to your opinion of my paper which differed considerably from my former boss in the Army.

Incidentally the proposed title of my book is: 'Experiencing the War Years: A Psychologist's Writings, Ponderings and Personal Journey During the Second American War with Iraq'...

Your input is valued. Please keep all of this under your hat, as I am paddling out on uncharted waters. Hope all is well with you."

Once again, this colleague currently employed by the Naval Academy brought a "listening ear" and much needed illumination to my self-imposed predicament. He noted, *"Sorry for the very long delay here. I am on sabbatical this year and only go into the office about once a month. I have also been terrible about checking and responding to e-mail... It has been good to have some time off to write and hang out with the kids.*

I don't think there is any problem including excerpts from our e-mail conversations Mark. I would ask that you let me peek at the final chapter just to correct anything I didn't express very well the first time. Otherwise, go for it.

Sorry this has created such a hassle for you. I shouldn't think publishing a book will be a major issue Mark. My experience is that there is a lot of storm and bluster and threatening that goes on around this issue, but when the rubber meets the road, you have very little to fear. You do have freedom of speech to some extent and unless your writing directly undermines the mission (unlikely to say the least) or slanders someone, or gives away secrets, etc..., there is little cause for concern - would try to both stay on reserve (you've worked long and hard) AND publish!"

His words of encouragement were not the ones I wanted to hear. Life would be so much simpler to sever the ties with the Army. I could then speak out without any danger of a backlash where my loyalty and obedience to the military could be questioned. Staying in would only complicate my life and create a host of anxieties as to when I would be confronted and criticized by those in the chain of command.

My personality is not geared to deal with ongoing ambiguous situations. Having a clear picture of what can be expected from others is much more manageable than the alternative. It really is not in my nature to purposely place myself in the limelight in order to become a potential target. This I am all to glad to defer to others more adventurous. It has been more in keeping with my nature to exhibit a strong tendency to perform Army tasks with as much dedication and service as possible – the gist being the fulfillment of a "model soldier" role. Going the "extra mile" had been inextricably woven into my character, and serving with distinction the natural outcome.

My colleague's words nevertheless resonated with my own

leanings in terms of salvaging my military career. He had simply helped to crystallize in my mind the idea of a paradigm shift where the two opposing actions were not so mutually exclusive as previously thought. Perhaps there really could be room in the military for soldiers like myself who were less than conventional. Could it be that an officer, or enlisted soldier, might exercise some independence of thought, even publicly, and yet remain committed to the military mission at hand? This kind of risk taking may in fact be an essential piece of what is needed in military circles to preserve some degree of democratic values, higher ethics challenging "group think," and creative problem solving helpful in achieving successful missions.

When I first arrived at my unit with the 82nd Airborne Division in 1973, I had the good fortune of being assigned to the Battalion Headquarters S-2 shop (i.e. Intelligence section). The individual in charge of the three-person shop was an intelligence officer by training and job specialty. He stood out like a "sore thumb" in a headquarters comprised of infantry officers. He also exhibited some rather odd interpersonal mannerisms which gave him the appearance of being somewhat effeminate and ill prepared for the rigors of combat. He also would irritate these officers to no end with his willingness to socially engage with enlisted soldiers as well as officers, and to tell some "steamy" jokes that were quite foreign to the "dirty" jokes of the other officers.

But, he had a superb intellect and was prone to conduct brilliant analysis of enemy forces and how best to prepare for engaging with them. His approach was like a direct affront to the more masculine and brawny style of the other officers at headquarters.

If there was ever a choice of which officer to go to war with, I would not have hesitated in picking this S-2 officer over all the others. He was not out to egotistically prove his superiority and leadership skills, but rather to approach each battle scenario with as much careful analysis as could be mustered. He was akin to a free thinker amongst other officers conditioned by training and personality to act according to the dictates of the group and minimal risk to one's own reputation.

Needless to say, he was reviled by the other officers and endlessly ridiculed. Since I was an extension of the officer I worked for, some of this disdain was directed my way as well. The negative attitudes toward this S-2 officer were manifested full force when the commander gave him a less than stellar "officer evaluation report" – this being equivalent to the "kiss of death." Yes, this single action proved to be the one which would facilitate his departure from the Army for good through a mechanism called "rifting." As I see it, the day he left the Army, the military as a whole lost the best kind of soldier, and one very difficult to replicate.

So, the decision has finally been reached for the time being. I will not voluntarily surrender my commission as an officer. My status as a Reserve psychologist will instead be maintained in an Army system pockmarked with irregularities. A concerted effort will be made to walk the "tightrope" – one hovering between humaneness and free speech on the one side and loyalty to country and mission on the other. For now, inner strength permitting, I will strive to meet the negative "flak" regarding my espoused views when, and if, it comes my way. In the midst of such a lofty enterprise, and perhaps when feeling particularly vulnerable, the character of the S-2 officer will once again come into focus, granting me another surge of courage to face the onslaught.

References
Solaro, E. **Retired Generals Rising up Against Iraq War**, Seattle Post Intelligencer,April 16, 2006.

AFTERWORD

The world is in a great historic struggle over this question of war and peace. Some of us see that it can't be solved by condemning war, but only by creating a more vivid and more vital way to live without shooting (Egendorf, 1985, p. 266).

A lot of ground has been covered for many since September 11th 2001. This has certainly been true in my case. I am no longer the same soldier, and "rookie" officer, that I was when the twin towers and a portion of the Pentagon were destroyed. My seasoning, although not the result of direct exposure to combat, occurred through my contact with other soldiers who provided often graphic depictions of the battleground in Iraq and to a lesser extent Afghanistan. It also has been due to the degree of attention I have given this war, and to the unique situations I have experienced which in different ways related to this war.

Being closer at hand to some of the military issues involved in conducting combat operations against the Taliban in Afghanistan, the Iraqi Army, and later the mounting insurgency in Iraq has fostered strong sentiments that have left their mark on me to this day. For a year in Germany, I found myself sucked into the vortex of the war and unable to extract myself. After all, I was an integral part of the organization carrying out wartime operations, and regularly in contact with those who still practically carried the sand in their boots, parched skin from a desert sun, and often horrific mental images of human suffering and death.

Issues had cropped up not of my choosing, ones providing

different observation points into the military system. These disturbing problems - whether it be freedom of speech, humane treatment of prisoners, or proper psychological care of soldiers and families - to name but a few, were serious matters that I could not ignore or wish away. I felt compelled to address these in a way that would honor those being impacted. As I related to one senior officer, I considered it my duty as an officer and human being on this planet to address these aspects of military life that had come across my radar screen in a big way.

But, in assuming some responsibility for these problem areas, I had to come to terms with the negative fallout I might encounter. Much as it went against the grain, I had to step out onto exposed ground without any cover or place to hide.

Doing this might lead some fellow soldiers to view my actions negatively, perhaps in a similar vein to those who purposely engage in bizarre actions counter to standard military bearing. In these cases however they were often doing this in an attempt to be discharged from the Army as unfit, kind of like "Klinger" in the television series, "MASH." My aim conversely was to remain in the military while at the same time promoting greater levels of honest and free expression of ideas, and humane treatment of both enemy and friendly forces.

In a very real way, my experiences during the war have sharpened my thoughts about the merits of a democracy, and the many ways democratic values can be undermined by even its strongest adherents. But, as history has shown, many in our own country have paid a high price to advocate for the kind of freedom and tolerance our country has imperfectly supported. I have come to appreciate that even great societies like ours have opposing forces to democratic values that can gain the upper hand. It is then incumbent upon a chorus of voices within our shores to make themselves heard on behalf of those being mistreated and on behalf of those ideals sprayed all over the constitution and declaration of independence we hold dear, even at times when there are many amongst us who would prefer a singular position and a stifling of any opposition.

The military happens to be one notable domain of our society which is inclined toward an authoritarian model of leadership and governance. It is a system that does not undergo major alterations easily, even though I have been witness to some prodigious changes over the course of my military career – the greater role of women soldiers being a prime example. One would be hard pressed to find a major institution in our society where democratic values collide more fiercely with authoritarian ones than within the armed forces.

But, it is precisely in this minefield, one where rank and unflinching obedience to designated command are so prominent, that a vulnerability emerges which undermines its so-called inner strength. Such unwavering loyalty to one's leaders (i.e. the chain of command) and willingness to defer to their judgment deprives individuals from personal responsibility, decision making and vocalized views or opinions.

In actuality, there are many soldiers who exercise a combination of both sides within the confines of their own units. This is partly dependent on the flexibility of squad, platoon and company wide leadership. Still, when greater issues are at stake, the military can ratchet up rapidly and exhibit a dogmatic and non-negotiable stance on any number of things. It is this tendency which can literally short circuit the vital input from subordinates, leading to command decisions that may turn out to have abysmal results. It may also lend support to a numbing of ethical decision making by those on the bottom level, and a kind of excessive control, faulty choices and narcissistic arrogance higher up the ladder.

There is a bottom line that cannot be avoided with military personnel. No amount of glossing things over – whether this be with comfortable housing, varied entertainment, fully equipped gyms, and the seemingly unlimited amenities for American soldiers – can escape the reality that ultimately the military's chief reason for existence is to inflict deadly harm to an identified enemy. Such acts of hostility are far from precise, leaving many noncombatants caught in the crossfire and scrambling for their very lives. All the tidying up efforts by the military ultimately fail to conceal the true nature of war and destruction to human life and property. However much there may be a need for armed forces ready and able to fight for its citizens and government, the overall cost is often so great as to even cause seasoned soldiers to question the worthiness of a wartime enterprise. As they often discover by first hand accounts, the achievement of military objectives can be very elusive and at times leave in their wake a Sherman-like "scorched earth" outcome.

I roll back in time to a period in my mid-twenties, being at the height of an idealistic streak in my life. In true maverick fashion, it had been my aim to establish beachheads along the Thai-Cambodian border where food supplies could be made available to Cambodian refugees.

The initial site selected was in a remote area in Northern Thailand where access was approved only by local military authority. Word had infiltrated into the interior of war-torn Cambodia that food supplies would soon be arriving at this border site. When a small contingent of us representing our relief organization showed up with a truckload of one hundred pound rice bags, we were greeted by approximately fifty expectant Cambodians. We were elated in witnessing the beginning of this much needed food supply depot to an area of

Cambodia absent of any relief efforts.

Our noble intention was to circumvent Thai Supreme Command by getting a new operation started without going through the typical bureaucratic morass Once well in place, the plan was to alert these authorities that a new site was fully operational and providing a valuable service – fait accompli.

Before our strategy could be acted upon, officials from Supreme Command showed up with some relief organization representatives to assess the potential for a new site in the northern tier of Thailand. Much to their surprise and embarrassment, these officials discovered our organization already there without their knowledge, and of course without any governmental sanction other than the local level. Supreme Command angrily responded to our presence by requiring us to leave the border area immediately.

Despite fervent appeals to Supreme Command, our organization was unsuccessful in getting the border operation reopened. The more disconcerting outcome of this refusal was that many starving Cambodians inside Cambodia would have continued to make the harrowing trek to this border site. If they managed to successfully evade marauding Khmer Rouge soldiers, they would then become potential victims to harassment or worse from Thai soldiers along that sector of the border. Their desperate hopes of receiving food supplies at the border, as previously reported, had been grievously dashed. Their own physical health was likely further weakened by the arduous journey to the border, and their return inland with empty stomachs possibly resulted in tragic consequences.

To this day, I struggle with haunting questions, droning on incessantly in my mind regarding this operation. Would it have been better for the Cambodian refugees involved if our operation had never existed, and they were simply left to their own struggles? Had our organization in its ignorance of the cultures they were involved with managed to incite a backlash effect much worse than the original predicament of low food supplies inside Cambodia? No easy answers emerge. What remains are the painful memories of an aborted operation and the troubling thoughts that our actions along the border produced untold human suffering, and an outcome far different from our humanitarian aims.

It is critical that we ask these same types of hard questions of our own military involvement in Iraq and Afghanistan. Our patriotic fervor should not deter us from seriously weighing the merits of the Iraq war in terms of the effects it has had on Iraqi or Afghani citizens, American soldiers, and others directly impacted by the war. This painful process of self-examination as a nation is really essential to deepen our insight, and to thus allow for alternative approaches to the conflict, if warranted. Such a public oriented discourse is truly the heartbeat of democracy and a necessary one to avoid slippage into more authoritarian modes of governance.

As I see it, a critical assessment of the war has been hindered by the contention that such challenges could undermine commitment to the troops. This kind of narrowly defined "oath of allegiance" has actually resulted in a devaluation of soldier needs for their own safety and wellbeing. It is as if the premise that, "the sacrifices made in this war have to be found worthwhile," are so politically loaded that opposing opinions take on un-American qualities. It does not seem to bode well for the American psyche to hold in one hand intrinsic meaningfulness for American casualities, and in the other hand deep reservations about the worthiness of the war effort as a whole.

The suspension of a vigorous democratic exchange in times of war, all in the name of unity and loyalty to flag, tends to consign the course of the war over to the hands of relatively few governmental leaders. In a sense, this leadership becomes a civilian extension of their military counterpart. An authoritarian leaning like this can lead to more free-wheeling combat with diminished checks and balances from others more inclined toward negotiation and avoidance of war. This is not a good thing in a free society that values competing views and opinions. It can also result in disastrous consequences like the needless annihilation of soldiers and noncombatants alike, whereas a more evenhanded approach might have spared countless lives.

At the tail end of World War II, the sinking of the U.S.S. Indianapolis by a Japanese submarine was one of the worst naval disasters of the entire war. Of the 1,196 men aboard, approximately 900 men ended up floating in the shark-infested waters of the Philippine Sea. When they were accidentally discovered four days later, there were only 316 who had survived the nightmarish ordeal (Newcomb, 2001).

One of the survivors was the ship's captain, Charles McVay III, who subsequently was court-martialed for alleged errors in judgment. Many of the survivors maintained that he had been wrongfully accused regarding his failure to place the ship on a zigzag course to better evade enemy attack. Their efforts to exonerate him were fruitless for over fifty years following the war (2001).

Vindication for Captain McVay took a major step forward in 1996 through a school research project by an eleven year old boy, Hunter Scott. He managed to send out questionnaires to many of the survivors of the Indianapolis' sinking, discovering there was unanimous agreement that the court-martial was unjustified (2001).

As a result of his dogged determination to get to the bottom of what really happened, his findings eventually ended up being heard in congressional hearings. He also provided evidence that Captain McVay had not been forewarned of another ship being sunk in the area prior to the ill-fated sinking of the Indianapolis. His findings suggested the Navy had not wanted to release needed information for fear of alerting the Japanese they had broken their enemy's communication codes (2001).

Following the lead of President Clinton, the Navy Department officially amended the record to clear Captain McVay's name in 2001. This was due in no small part to an impressionable boy's quest for justice (2001).

All of the combined wisdom within the Navy for a fifty year span could not find the right path to adjudicate the McVay case. Furthermore, the systemic shortcomings within the Navy could not be illuminated for what these were. Assigning blame to CPT McVay, as well as a few others held responsible for failure to notify proper authorities the ship was overdue at its designated arrival port, served to insulate the institution at much higher levels from culpability (2001).

It took a prepubescent boy to lead a highly irregular and unorthodox charge that resulted in compelling a rigid institution like the Navy to acknowledge a wrong done to one of their own. Even more spectacular because of Hunter Scott's age, he offers to the rest of us a model of "higher ethics" that is humbling by the intensity of its blinding radiance.

One has to wonder what someone of his caliber would be like if he was a member of the military, and how he would address injustice and improprieties within military circles. Would Mr. Scott remain in his "lane" and avoid any flak from his superiors when truthfulness seemed to be taking a pummeling?

Hypothetical situations are hard to predict in terms of an outcome. However Mr. Scott would have responded, he has been a tremendous source of inspiration for me in completing this book. His strength of character and resolve to find the truth has helped to confirm in my mind the value of my own endeavor.

It is my conviction the exercising of "free speech" while in the military is critically important to the overall mission, and to the welfare of soldiers at large. It is enough that many solders are being asked to place themselves in harm's way and to undergo many hardships. It seems unreasonable to also require these warriors to keep their opinions and thoughts about the war they are involved in private and out of the "public eye." Having some capacity to seriously assess the conduct of the war, and the merits of the specific missions their units are attempting to accomplish, is the kind of feedback loop which can assist in avoiding unnecessary mistakes and loss of life, as well as misguided strategic blunders.

Rieckhoff (2006) gives expression to the frustrations his unit felt about decisions that were beyond their control.

We were supposed to call up to our Battalion HQ, who decided whether or not to relay our messages. That was how they could "direct" the action on the ground from a safe, air-conditioned distance. To make matters worse, that unit was from a different Battalion than mine, and my Battalion's HQ probably did not even know their Battalion HQ's frequency. I wasn't even supposed to cross the sector line, walk over to the other unit and ask them what their frequency was. It was a complete bureaucratic muddle that reflected the fucked-up patchwork of units—Marines, Army, National Guard, British troops, contractors, circus clowns, what have you — that our brilliant leaders in Washington had thrown into this war (p.101).

Questioning the pros and cons of any war American soldiers are involved in is fully justified for all its citizens, as well as the rest of those making up the world community. We cannot rightfully call ourselves a true democratic society when endorsement of a given war is strongly expected in order to be considered a genuine patriot. Debate should in fact be encouraged and accepted every step of the way during a war effort. A given war may begin with extreme optimism and conviction to later be supplanted by disillusionment and uncertainty. Remaining fixed on a course of action in war, unswerving and relentlessly determined, can at times induce blindness to changing realities that alter the landscape of a conflict entirely. Soldiers understand this concept all too well, as flexibility and openness to rapidly altered circumstances is a necessity in order to survive to see another day.

Perhaps I am a soldier who has stumbled off course during this latest war. It could be that civilian life has rubbed off on me too much where the end result has been to become soft on the "thugs of the world." My psychological fitness to stoicly function as a disciplined soldier may be called into question in light of my ambivalence with the military lately and my excessive sympathies toward those traumatized by the fighting. Indeed I have lost my edge, if indeed I ever had it. All that remains is a queasy, sickening feeling in my stomach that cannot be consoled. This does seem to have all the typical markings of a "wayward soldier," one giving way to too much troubled thought to things that cannot be changed.

Try as I might, I have not been able to walk back into the civilian mainstream, unencumbered by a war fought halfway around the globe. I look for answers, but seem to always come up short. I cannot accept the fact that the dye is cast, and that it is inevitable and "cemented in concrete" for this war to proceed on the kind of "bloodbath" path it has been on. Stubbornly, I cling to high minded notions that alternative approaches to this present carnage exists in the realm of potential contingencies, and with just the right finesse could be activated.

In my search for an alternative approach to the war in Iraq where so much suffering and loss of life has occurred, I came across a program in Austria which really caught my attention. It was described as follows:

"We wish to invite you to join a select group of 45 students from around the world in an intensive course in peace and conflict studies at the European University Center of Peace Studies (EPU) in Stadtschlaining, Austria. All the courses are taught in English, by leading specialists in their field from around the world, including Johan Galtung, one of the founders of the academic discipline of peace research and frequent mediator in international conflict. Studying with the founder of a new academic discipline is a rare opportunity, like studying economics with Adam Smith. EPU offers students a well-rounded program covering Peace with Security, Development, Freedom, Nature and Culture.

The Program, established in 1991 by Dr. Gerald Mader, Founder and President of the Austrian Study Center for Peace and Conflict Resolution, received the 1995 UNESCO Prize for Peace Education.

In addition to attending courses, students get to know each other closely and conclude friendships that last a lifetime. In the fall of 2005, we had 43 students from 29 countries from four continents. Many former students said that studying at EPU was the best time of their life. Peace Studies are a highly interdisciplinary and growing academic field. Students who have successfully completed our program are well grounded in both theory and practice to face the challenges of global conflict and transformation. We are happy and proud that many of our former students now have thriving careers in international organizations, NGO's business, universities, or work with their governments."

It did not take a whole lot of thought in making the decision to apply for this semester of study in Austria. My e-mail to the European Peace University read as follows:

"My search for a peace studies program has now entered the third year. My aim has been to find a program brief enough to maintain my current work commitments. But, in addition, it has been important for me to discover a program covering the range of peace studies sufficiently to prepare me for practical work in the field of peace and conflict studies. I spent a year in Germany recently where I scoured the varied programs in Europe and the United States in an attempt to find the optimal match. European University Center for Peace Studies repeatedly caught my attention because of its broad international scope and solid scholastic reputation.

The program being offered appeals to my desire to be intellectually challenged in an area of study so closely tied to my own interests. I personally thrive in an academic environment with students and faculty representing so many varied perspectives and cultural backgrounds. It is my sense that whatever peace and conflict endeavors I might be involved with in the future will be fundamentally shaped by the quality of these peer interactions both in and outside the classroom. It strikes me as a rare combination to be exposed to the highest caliber of scholarship in the field along with such a stimulating experiential component. In my judgment these are academic features inherent to the semester program at Stadtschlaining.

I am confident the skills and knowledge gained from the program will equip me with a keener understanding of conflict issues throughout the world. It will also provide me the tools enhancing my own competency to work internationally. My capacity to effectively discern what projects to become involved in would be further developed, as well as the knowledge of appropriate mechanisms in establishing such commitments.

One of my greatest struggles with peace work to date has been the difficulty of finding assignments in this domain. The many interpersonal connections that would occur during the course of the program would very likely facilitate opportunities in the future to provide needed services and to gain practical experience. Thus, my humanistic driven desire to strive for peaceful and cooperative coexistence on this planet would assume more realistic outlets for working with others toward this end."

So, there is it. I am seeking for a kind of Hegelian synthesis between two apparent opposites, these being the role of a soldier and that of a peacemaker. Perhaps this is more fitting than it sounds at first. Who more than soldiers can comprehend the gruesome specter of war in all of its inconsistencies and nihilistic spasms? It is for solders to experience the jolting shock of human beings (i.e. enemy, friendly, and noncombatants) so quickly being reduced to "body parts" and to a state of nonexistence, at least with regard to this life on earth.

At least for some soldiers, such a harsh exposure can move them to a kinder and gentler disposition, and with a yearning to discover the qualities of all humans which can bind us together. And if tapped into early enough, having to kill or maim an identified enemy before witnessing the common humanity may be found to be unnecessary – that the highest calling of the soldier may be to lead the rest of us by example to a serene pasture where future wars are closer to extinction than ever before. If this is a sign of being "wayward" and off the beaten path, then I will just have to accept this identity with all the gusto of one who finds life an indescribable prize for all persons the world over, and one not to be easily desecrated or dehumanized.

References
Egendorf, A. (1985). <u>Healing from the war: Trauma and transformation after Vietnam</u>. Boston, MA: Shambhala Publications, Inc.

Rieckhoff, P. (2006). <u>Chasing ghosts: A soldier's fight for America from Baghdad to Washington</u>. London, England: Penguin Books Ltd.